T0167352

THE MEDIA SAVVY LEADER

VISIBILITY, INFLUENCE, AND RESULTS IN A COMPETITIVE WORLD

DAVID HENDERSON

Robert D. Reed Publishers • Bandon, OR

Robert D. Reed Publishers
P.O. Box 1992
Bandon, OR 97411
Phone: 541-347-9882; Fax: -9883
E-mail: 4bobreed@msn.com
Website: www.rdrpublishers.com

Editor: Laura Porter Hall of The Literary Spa
Cover Designer: Cleone Lyvonne
Photographer: "CEO on Learjet 45," © Ed Lallo
Interior Designer: Amy Cole

ISBN 13: 978-1-934759-20-2
ISBN 10: 1-934759-20-1

Library of Congress Number: 2008934687

*Manufactured, Typeset, and Printed in the
United States of America*

For Kit
My wife, best friend and partner, today and beyond

CONTENTS

CONTENTS

INTRODUCTION

How many times have you wondered how the leaders of some companies and organizations get so much terrific media coverage—the kind that influences sales or boosts funding or heightens customer and shareholder excitement—while others fail, even though they might have a good story?

During three decades as a professional communications strategist and journalist, I have admired and studied the leaders among us who have the ability to make things happen by capturing the spotlight of the most powerful form of communications in the world—the news media.

Are people born with such natural charisma or is it a talent cultivated through an awareness of what sparks our attention and imagination? I will leave the former for psychologists to debate. But I am convinced that people can learn the secrets of charisma and become outstanding, savvy communicators, even when standing before a horde of reporters with a battery of microphones, cameras, and harsh lights.

I admit that I have watched with astonishment and envy as the darlings of the media repeatedly get what seems to be more than their share of fabulous coverage. The question is, how do they pull it off?!

The news media is unquestionably the most important and effective form of communication in today's world; it is certainly becoming more effective at reaching broad audiences than traditional advertising. Leaders are made, reputations altered, good deeds acknowledged, misdeeds exposed, the unknown becomes legend, and memories formed among vast audiences—all through stories in the media.

While the media's reach is ever expanding, it is also changing dramatically. Even the practice of brand management, which was once a marketing discipline, is now more expeditiously achieved by innovative and sustained communications through the media and online.

The whole face of what we know as the media is rapidly changing with the explosive credibility and influence of new media outlets, such as Politico.com, ProPublica, the Investigative Reporter Workshop, and the Center for Independent Media.

With the advent of such New Media, made possible by the online digital revolution, we seemingly have infinite ways to find news and information at our fingertips, and we can explore new ways of having our voices be heard. We care less today about what someone is pushing at us and more about our own personal choices—a trend that has turned the whole world of marketing and advertising upside down.

The days of massive spending on advertising campaigns to debut new products or ideas are waning and quickly becoming history. Generating influence today requires clever exposure across the diverse and evolving channels of the traditional news media together with a savvy use of New Media, including blogs, podcasts, social networking, streaming video, and engaging people in conversations online.

It is no surprise, then, that corporations and organizations today are scrambling to understand how to create effective communications in today's complex digital world of instantaneous deadlines and growing tactical ways to reach journalists, bloggers, and the burgeoning popularity of online interactivity and social communities.

There has been a flurry of excitement over the ever-evolving tools of the digital revolution. Should you launch a blog? How about podcasts? What are the merits a special wiki to explain a technical industry or complex issues? What about the plethora of online services that promise to deliver your press release into the hands of thousands of reporters?

How do you make intelligent choices about what works and what does not? Let us start by stepping back and taking a more strategic view of the competitive landscape. Let's put aside for a moment all the tactical choices for—things like interactive sites, streaming video, viral word-of-mouth tactics, social networks, branding in a virtual world, Web site newsrooms, blogs, and so on—to focus on understanding what's behind becoming a media savvy leader, and the strategic elements that include objectives, perspective, understanding audiences, messages, and outcomes.

What do you, as a leader, want to achieve by using the media to promote your message? How can you best manage communications through the media to gain assurance that your words are being conveyed accurately? How can you manage interactions with journalists and bloggers to your advantage? On a personal level, how can you become media savvy and recognized as an influential and respected voice in your competitive field? You will find the answers and solutions you are seeking in this book.

I have never thought there was any magic to getting good media coverage for my clients.

An executive at top public relations agency once told me that media relations—the way you communicate your story to the news media in hopes of seeing it in print or online or on-the-air—was a science. I, however, disagree.

Savvy media leadership, the kind that delivers the results you desire, is not magic; it certainly is not science or even an art. It is an imperfect, ever-evolving craft, at best. But it can be extremely powerful.

The practice of influential communications with the media comes from knowing what makes a news story, identifying the best news outfit to reach your audiences, finding a reporter who agrees with you about the story, and working with the reporter to develop a story with which you will be pleased. The goal is to reach and motivate audiences.

My desire is for this book to deliver valuable answers and perspective, which I derived largely from compiling the viewpoints of hundreds of working journalists—many well known—as well as my own three-decade experience in media communications. If you want to get your story noticed by the news media, it only makes sense to have reporters and editors give some insider tips.

The Media Savvy Leader details how to shape information, deliver messages, enhance distinctive brand recognition, and achieve desired influence in today's competitive New Media world. This book provides a candid look at why some leaders are high-profile media stars who generate outstanding results while others are relegated to stand in the shadows.

In researching this book, I interviewed dozens of business, association, and non-profit leaders along with more than 150 working journalists—the gatekeepers of the mainstream news media's massive power and the evolving New Media of the digital revolution.

You can achieve significant success if you're smart, fast on your feet, understand the media's playing field, and know how to control your message. For example, you can boost brand awareness for an organization, prominently position a product or service, provide clear and accurate information in a crisis, and help to right a wrong, among other desired results. Because of the near-instant credibility and widespread audience reach that comes with news coverage, media relations can be the most influential tool in an organization's marketing strategy.

When I made the career jump from network news correspondent at CBS News to founder and managing partner of a strategic communications firm, it seemed only natural for me to begin building effective media relations for my clients by figuring out a news angle that would appeal to a particular reporter.

But over the intervening years, I realized that few executives and public relations people ever consider what a reporter needs for a story. Even fewer have ever bothered to invest the time to develop working relationships with the news media, preferring instead to send news releases indiscriminately to as many journalists as possible.

When I began to teach classes on image and reputation management at the University of Virginia in the late 1990s, I found that it was most effective to explain the subtleties of how audience perceptions are formed, influenced and redirected today to achieve desired outcomes, including an inside peek at how the media business works.

I was, however, faced with a dilemma: I wanted a book to share with students but could find nothing—university-level textbook or otherwise—that had even a hint of recognition of the media's needs, especially from a journalist's perspective.

The books I found—including recent ones—seemed to range from one extreme to another. They were either from a bygone era of media relations or they attempted to shill tactical technology solutions, such as blogs, as a way to solve all your image issues. They avoided the importance of strategic positioning and clear messages to create influence.

The Media Savvy Leader takes a different approach that begins with an insider's perspective on the latest ways leaders are made and recognized in today's hot media world.

We no longer live in a time when you could *push* something at the media and expect them to pay attention. Instead, the media today is a fiercely competitive business that pays news people to find fresh, new stories—the more sensational, the better.

We are witnessing a seismic transformation of power in the news industry that is—according to the Project for Excellence in Journalism at Columbia University—influenced by the dynamics of technology; audience shifts, changing revenue streams, and the always present, never-ending news cycles. I heard the impact of these changing dynamics expressed over and over by people in the news business as I researched this book. They used these exact words— seismic change—to describe this shift in the news industry, which affects anyone who hopes to get a story in a newspaper or magazine, online, or on the air. Not surprisingly, many traditional methods of getting journalists' attention no longer work.

The old, traditional tools of media relations—news releases and news conferences—are fast becoming obsolete. Today's media doesn't have the time to mess with that stuff, preferring instead to rely on trusted sources, relationships, online resources, and, most of all, exclusivity.

So this book is a first: a practical field guide on how to capture your share of the spotlight in front of the media and then effectively deliver your news and messages in a manner that boosts the value of your organization—and your own success at the same time—in the Internet age.

There is one caveat, however, to becoming a media savvy leader in today's world—it requires an investment of your own time and involvement. Being a leader who captures the media's attention is not something that can be delegated.

You may not have been born with the natural charisma of a great communicator, but you sure can develop skills to become a darn good one. *The Media Savvy Leader* delivers the insight to:

- Capture the media's attention when the time is right.

- Communicate your vision clearly and accurately.

- Enhance your image, reputation, and brand value.

- Establish trusted working relationships with key journalists.

- Evaluate which new online technology tool is most effective.

- Achieve accurate, credible, and tangible results that meet your objectives.

Whether used in building a brand, marketing a product or service, or promoting an image, knowledge of how the media turns facts into news and what the media looks for in a story will give you a significant competitive edge. This tool of knowledge will help you achieve a clear and distinct voice in a world filled with cluttered messages.

David Henderson
Arlington, Virginia

PART ONE

GAIN INFLUENCE AMID NOISE, HYPE, AND POWER

CHAPTER ONE

THE VALUE OF AN INFLUENTIAL VOICE

There are important voices that gain trust and change how business is done worldwide. We hear the voices and of these highly successful leaders and executives who use the awesome power of the news media to build trust in the brand value of their corporations, activist groups, associations, and non-governmental organizations—people like Richard Branson … Steve Jobs … Oprah Winfrey … Layli Miller-Muro … Robert Iger … Bill Gates.

These select few generate media coverage that is usually reserved for rock stars, only they are far more grounded and credible. They also enhance their own image, worth, and the way we view and respect them as leaders.

The list of people who authentically know the value of a clear, influential voice is exclusive—astonishingly short, in fact—which begs the question: How do *these* people enrapture audiences, capture the attention of reporters, and command such enormous coverage?

You may not recognize Ms. Miller-Muro's name among Branson, Jobs, Oprah, or the others, but she is clearly a leading communicator in the not-for-profit world, as I will explain a little later.

These leaders all share common threads of skill as great communicators, including the exceptional ability to get to the point—the true purpose of their message—quickly, clearly, and in simple words so that we stop what we are doing to listen, understand, and believe what they say.

These savvy few also know that successful image leadership requires planning, the integration of all levels of their organizations, and their own engagement in behaving as an authentic leader. Why? Because too much is at stake—the value of managing an organization's reputation is too important to be delegated.

Successful leaders have examined—at one time or another, each in his or her own way—a critical reality of successful leadership in today's media driven world:

Protecting a reputation begins with understanding the implications and potential cost of not protecting a reputation.

These people know that, according to research on the importance of brand management, roughly 82 percent of shareholder value is intangible. It's merely a perception, impression, or … *feeling* that people have about their brands. As such, these leaders are keenly aware that reputations can be injured with a single misstep.

They also know that the investment to protect a reputation is infinitely less than the expense needed to fix one that is damaged, sometimes by self-inflicted mistakes.

Savvy leaders have taken the time—as leaders in their respective fields—to understand how the media works. As newsmakers, they know what to say and how to deliver their messages so that reporters will pay attention and will most often write positive stories.

Such leaders know that reporters look for sound bites and quotable quotes—not lengthy explanations—so they get to their point quickly when communicating their messages. They concisely and clearly articulate the vision of their respective organizations in a way that excites people and creates positive results.

Although these leaders have support staff, they have not delegated the voice of their organizations to others. They not only deliver communications but also put a face on their organizations. We, as a public and an audience, immediately recognize these leaders and trust what they say.

Captivating leaders know that in today's highly competitive world, successful endeavors become even more successful when they reflect the personality and charisma of the person at the helm. They also know that the way that person behaves in the public spotlight is key.

While Richard Branson does not run all of the 350 companies under his Virgin brand, it is his individual image and voice that brings each of them to life. With the magnificent grace and timing of a symphony conductor, Branson captures terrific and consistent media coverage.

Oprah Winfrey is unique—she is the brand, the product, the center of her successful universe and its communicator. Everything is all about Oprah, all of the time—from Oprah's book club to *Oprah* magazine to Oprah programs to build schools.

Winfrey's strategic formula is genuine, connects passionately with a sizable loyal audience, and works to make things happen. She often creates her own news, always in a manner that embraces her fans and respects the projects to which she lends her name. When not communicated through her own media channels, including a news magazine-style Web site and *Oprah* magazine, Winfrey's stories pull the mainstream news media like a magnet, due in large measure to her celebrity.

Few successfully identify the magic key to unlock access to the world of Oprah and attract her interest. But Oprah's endorsement is golden. Thousands of people go knocking on her door yet only a few actually get to stand in the warm spotlight with her.

Leaders like Branson and Winfrey know that the power of reaching large audiences is frequently accessed through credible and popular appeal of news media coverage. They are also aware that the influence of traditional advertising in today's world has been greatly diminished, partly due to all the media choices at our fingertips and the competitive clutter created by the confluence of traditional and New Media. News coverage today has never been more influential.

Most of all, effective leaders know that getting media coverage is a clever form of *storytelling*. The traditional, tactical approach of *pushing* things—press releases, legal-sounding statements, promotional materials—*at* reporters no longer works. Quite the contrary, the secret to capturing the media's attention in today's world is having an alluring story to tell.

So, what do today's most influential leaders have in common? Storytelling is one leading shared trait.

Today's successful leaders have the skills to communicate corporate messages and unique perspectives through clever stories that capture our attention, involve us in what seems like exclusive insight into their vision for the future, and motivate us to action. Magnetic leaders generate great news coverage because they give journalists exactly what they desire—a compelling story.

Watch these leaders closely: While in the media's glare, they introduce new products, services, or ideas by sharing captivating stories. They speak in quotable quotes—a few short and appealing words that are precisely the sort of thing that reporters listen for and, in fact, need to develop stories.

We watch, listen, read, and get excited about their messages because these leaders share their stories with *us*. They make us feel special, and we view them as authentic leaders of the best kind.

Influential leaders get right to the point and explain about often-complex issues in simple terms so we all can understand. After all, they are sharing a story with us that excites them; we can sense and share in their enthusiasm and passion. They are not afraid of having a sense of humor, showing humility, or being human. We admire them, relate to them, and believe we understand what they are saying. In most cases, our positive perception of the companies or organizations they lead increases.

Most of all, such leaders accept responsibility and accountability. We—and the media—trust them and the brands they represent.

While doing research for this book, I spoke not only with many successful journalists who talked about today's most interesting leaders and provided an insider's perspective on the latest trends in communications, but I also interviewed outstanding leaders of corporations, non-profits, and associations who are recognized for being credible, transparent, and media savvy.

In addition to their storytelling ability, these leaders also share an understanding that in today's world—which is full of hype and message clutter—they need to get to the point clearly and quickly when they have something to say. They use words that all of us understand—words that are also free of jargon, clichés, acronyms, and bravado.

The stories savvy leaders present are structured like a pyramid. Think about the image of a pyramid—a point at the top that expands downward to a broad base. When speaking with reporters, they get to the point first and then provide greater understanding through anecdotes, facts, and examples. The best stories are short, sweet, and framed to appeal to our logic and emotion.

Telling compelling, structured stories is the most effective way to connect with audiences on a more personal and trusted level. Such stories involve and embrace audiences while discretely underscoring our own reputation and what is special about what we are saying. Through a story, we can credibly communicate important yet intangible issues, such as why the audience should value or care about a product, service, or cause. We can subtly position ourselves as a trusted partner to share a vision or quest with an audience and, in the process, achieve lasting competitive leadership.

And, then, there is the timely and relevant issue of what today's savvy leader must know about using the Internet to communicate.

Billionaire entrepreneur Mark Cuban, chairman of HDNet Television and owner of the Dallas Mavericks, is known for his candid perspective and his savvy use of the Internet. He believes that today's leaders must accept the responsibility and take charge of learning how to communicate online. Either that, or he warns, "The Internet will do it for them, and it won't be pretty."

Taking control of media and communications opportunities, whether mainstream or online, and using them for your advantage is certainly not the exclusive purview of media superstars. It is essential for any leader or executive who hopes to be heard in today's world.

This book is for executives of companies, associations, non-governmental entities, and not-for-profit organizations who recognize that favorable media coverage can bring valuable benefits in the form of awareness, influence, sales, members, support, fund-raising, goodwill, and competitive advantage. The following chapters are intended for anyone who wants to become an authentic leader in communications. Savvy knowledge of how to use the news media can make a good brand even better. Readers will find profound insight into the distinctive techniques of making news—both for themselves and the organizations they represent. Their voices will be clear and heard and respected.

CHAPTER TWO

VISIONARY LEADERSHIP IN THE INTERNET AGE

Bill Gates of Microsoft and Steve Jobs of Apple—two icons of technology—have appeared together on numerous occasions before audiences of journalists who cover the software and computer industries (and anyone else fortunate enough to slip in). Despite a natural impulse to "talk tech" to the tech reporters, Jobs and Gates do exactly what I mentioned in the previous chapter: They smartly discuss issues and reply to questions in language all of us understand. They have cultivated a gift to distill highly technical concepts and issues into simple, easy to understand statements.

Why? Well, it is quite simple—they view and respect the role of reporters as conduits who will carry their words and perspective about new products and industry developments to much broader audiences, including you and me. They also know there is nothing to be gained by talking over our heads.

Gates and Jobs communicate clearly and masterfully on an individual basis with reporters, whether a roomful or just a few. Reporters—through the news organizations they represent—wield influence to carry forward the image of charisma, leadership, and excitement in your words.

Jobs' persuasiveness stems from his personal certainty in his beliefs. When he speaks of an Apple product, for example, you begin to believe that it is the greatest device ever created because Steve Jobs believes it is so. His transparency may seem like a crippling liability, but it is actually a strength.

Here's another secret: The messages of today's most effective communicators are interwoven throughout all levels of their organizations to enhance understanding, excitement in the company's mission, respect for the intelligence of leadership, and, ultimately, the brand image. It is like a beacon that clarifies understanding and builds consensus.

An effective media strategy may begin with a terrific coverage angle that gets our attention, but that's only part of a contemporary strategic approach to communications. As mentioned previously, an authentic leader's interface with the media must be reflected throughout the organization's promotion and marketing matrix. Each dynamic of the leader's vision and message are told, retold, and threaded seamlessly into the organization's communications—online, streaming video, podcasts, visually, in-stores, print, blogs, all of which can be types of advertising. Even the style in which employees interact personally with stakeholders, customers, and vendors should be seamlessly woven into communications. This holistic approach increases impact, controls favorable perceptions, and delivers successful results. Such a style even reaches and excites the financial crowd on Wall Street. It all begins with a captivating story that is communicated by the person at the top—a story that then trickles down and excites the entire organization.

What makes a keynote address or news conference by Steve Jobs, in particular, so compelling is that his opinions translate directly into Apple's policies and products. Jobs consistently demonstrates his extraordinary merging of unique management and communication styles. One person, not even a visionary CEO like Jobs, can control every detail of every product, but Jobs has proven his willingness to reach all the way down the organizational chart and make decisions about even the smallest features. His readiness to roll up his shirtsleeves and exert control and leadership over anything makes the legendary idea that he controls everything seem ... well, reasonable.

As one Jobs observer noted, "His tendency to micromanage can more charitably be viewed as a refreshing willingness to cut through bureaucracy. Few 'insanely great' products are created by committees, after all."

When Jobs makes a statement, everyone at Apple—from sales people in retail outlets worldwide to technical and customer support experts at call centers—not only learn the news at near-light speed but comprehend his vision and how it translates into the company's unique style. Not surprisingly, the brightness of their enthusiasm shines from within the company and helps Jobs inspire the world.

Job's leadership style is a dramatic change from the traditional leadership style at most organizations, which seem haphazard or lame by comparison. Few executives invest significant time and energy venturing into the dusty corners of their organizations to inspire greatness. Even fewer work to avoid bureaucracy. When it comes to communicating messages, the traditional and commonly accepted attempts to get media attention—for example, by distributing prepared and sterile-sounding statements that have been edited by attorneys, department heads, supervisors, and PR people—and their associated results often are disappointing. They simply are not in the same class as companies like Apple.

Another reason today's great communicators are so successful is that their messages are truthful, timely, and consistent.

"Sixteen years on *Face The Nation* has taught me one thing," CBS newsman Bob Schieffer told me. "When I ask a question and guests start laying out conditions such as 'first let me tell you' or 'the real questions is' or 'it is important to put that in context,' I know we're headed down the old rabbit trail that will take us anywhere but to a straight answer.

"When people want to answer, they do so quickly, directly, and clearly. When they don't, we get all those conditions and lectures about the importance of context," he said.

Schieffer, a veteran Washington, D.C., journalist, was expressing his frustration at the Bush administration's reversal regarding new conditions for the release of a long-waited report on progress in Iraq.

"Maybe it's because I've been dragged down the old rabbit trail too many times by too many people with something to hide," Schieffer said, "but this doesn't sound like we're headed to a straight answer. No, this sounds like anything but."

Schieffer was saying that he, like any other working journalist, expects truth and straight answers, without equivocation, when he asks a question of a newsmaker—no stalling or dancing away from the subject.

Of course, what Schieffer expects from a newsmaker and what he gets is not always the same thing.

During my career as a network journalist and then a communications strategist, I cannot begin to list the examples of chief executives of companies who demanded great media coverage but looked with disdain at any interface with the media. Such executives don't trust the media, belittle reporters, and treat interaction with the media as an intrusion. Yet they expect great media coverage and heads will roll if they don't get it.

When I was a news correspondent, some executives went so far as to threaten to call my boss if they didn't like a story. Although that was a few years ago, executives like that continue to run companies and continue to see the media as adversaries.

When such executives stand in front of microphones and speak on behalf of their organizations, they often appear wooden, flat, and, well ... boring. It is as if these executives communicate in riddles and fail to get to the point. On occasion, these executives' body language suggest they would prefer to drink battery acid than meet with the press. When a reporter asks a question, their responses either wander, sound too rehearsed, or appear even hostile. The result is that no one really cares about the message—including the media.

"I have been amazed sometimes," Gary Shapiro said, "by the inability of a CEO not only to deal with the media, but to articulate a sentence."

Shapiro is president and chief executive of the powerful and high profile Consumer Electronics Association (CEA) that has more than 2,100 member companies.

So, what's the difference between an effective and ineffective communicator? How do people like Branson, Jobs, Oprah, Iger, Miller-Muro, and Gates become so media savvy and are, in some cases, treated like revered celebrities by the media while others never come close and stand forever in the shadows of obscurity? Although several qualities have already been shared, important secrets from leading journalists and other insiders follow.

In the vast world of trade associations, CEA's Shapiro is recognized as a dynamic and visionary communicator who knows how to capitalize on media opportunities. One of his primary responsibilities is to speak on behalf of the enormous and diverse industry he represents and he has earned a good reputation in an industry where the brand of a company is largely formed by media coverage—coverage that is greatly influenced by the charisma, passion, and communications skills of the person at the helm.

Each year, the Consumer Electronics Association stages the largest trade show of its type in the world—The Consumer Electronics Show or CES—that is attended by 140,000 people who want an early peek at the newest, latest, and coolest products and gadgets in the electronics industry. The Consumer Electronics Show is also the biggest annual press event in the world.

For corporate leaders, an opportunity to speak at CES is highly coveted. Chief executive officers and their lieutenants often lobby Shapiro's office for months for a slot in the program; one of Shapiro's responsibilities is to evaluate how well a CEO communicates.

Yet, surprisingly, in today's highly competitive world—a world in which good communications skills are necessary for leadership—not all chief executives have the ability to articulate a vision for their company or to deliver a clear, lucid message whether to a large audience during a speech or to one reporter during an interview. In fact, quite a few cannot, and it reflects badly on their organizations.

"How do you become to be a CEO of a major company when you cannot speak publicly?" Shapiro exclaimed as we met in his Arlington, Virginia, office. "I have wondered how a board makes a decision like that (to hire such a person)."

From a purely practical perspective, a great speaker at CES not only captures invaluable media coverage for his or her own company, but the value of the trade show itself is enhanced.

Several corporate leaders, including Robert Iger of Disney, have used a speaking opportunity at CES to recalibrate corporate vision, shake off old perceptions, and competitively reposition the images of their organizations. Stock prices often jump as a result of their visibility, direction, and confidence.

When a leader articulates the corporate vision behind a new product, initiative, or service and receives glowing reviews by respected journalists, the whole company benefits from sales, customer satisfaction, brand awareness, and enhanced shareholder value.

The value of media coverage today has in many cases become

exponentially greater and even more credible than advertising, and at a fraction of the cost of paid ads. The credibility of authentic messages in plain language win out over the predictable and tired clichés of advertising.

On the broader canvas of issues that impact lives of people around the globe, understanding today's melding of traditional and New Media with online technology has never been more important.

In the world of human rights, personal and religious freedoms, and equality, media coverage or a responsibly written blog can make the difference, sometimes even between life and death.

Yet, not-for-profit organizations and corporations alike frequently struggle to find ways to get the media's attention. They often lack expertise and contacts to reach out at the right time, with the right story angle and message, and to the right people in the media who can make a difference.

Here's another secret: Great media coverage starts with the person at the top owning a big piece of the responsibility for understanding and practicing the insider secrets for how to make it happen. It is a responsibility that requires constant attention and a meaningful investment of time. But the rewards of enhanced leadership charisma, a highly motivated team, and a more exciting vision and image for the organization make it worthwhile.

Hiring a public relations agency for support is not always a solution for reasons I will discuss in detail in a subsequent chapter. Many public relations agencies simply have not invested in the latest methods of working with today's ever-changing media and prefer, instead, to write press releases that are distributed indiscriminately to vast numbers of journalists who generally will not pay attention to them. Press releases have become the least effective way of getting the media's attention. Nevertheless, such tactics help to maximize agency billable hours and profits.

Leaders must create timely, sharp, and relevant stories that appeal to the media, as well as stakeholders; they must also employ unique methods to get messages to the right people in the media and to create favorable news for their organizations or themselves.

We must remember the competition we face everyday, in whatever we do. We live in a fiercely competitive world in which many people clamber to get attention before a news media that has been financially damaged by the digital revolution and New Media upstarts, while losing revenue sources and ever-changing audiences. We live in a world where even venerable institutions, like the *New York Times*, compete for audience revenue with the latest evolving online phenomena like YouTube and Facebook.

In a New Media age, traditional Web sites may appear static and boring. We must consider the effectiveness of new tools of communications, such as blogs, vlogs (video blogs), and wikis. Should your chief executive have a blog? Should funds be invested in building brand awareness within cyber worlds, like Second Life? How can the new technology of New Media work to enhance visibility for your organization and provide a more compelling and active image online?

All cool bells and whistles of technology aside, the secrets to accurately communicating news and generating great media attention in this new world order for reaching audiences may sound a little old-fashioned, but are astonishingly effective:

- Take responsibility, as a leader, for being the face and voice of your organization.

- Create visionary messages that people will find captivating.

- Communicate your messages through a clever story. A good story is precisely want the media wants.

- Get to the point—quickly and clearly—using words we all understand.

- Interweave your messages throughout all levels of your organization, like a beacon shining on a path to enhance understanding.

- Be consistent, timely, truthful, and relevant in your messages.

- Avoid talking about your organization but rather talk about the value of what your organization does.

These points do not really look like great secrets, after all, do they?! Each point is simply common sense that respects how today's news media functions in a New Media world. These techniques capture superb and favorable media coverage that reach vast audiences. The odd part is that most companies and organizations remain mired in worn-out, threadbare tactics and dysfunctional internal politics that hinder the growth of a company's image, reputation, and brand. It's time for a refreshing change.

There are forces of change actively churning within the business of strategic communications, the news industry, and the New Media. These forces are and created by ever-changing technology that is also changing how we must approach and work with journalists to get our story reported, today and into the future.

It is clear that anyone who practices effective strategic communications must keep pace with the changing media and embrace new methods.

Perhaps no person has left a greater and more positive imprint on the practice of strategic communications worldwide over the last couple of decades than the late Michael Deaver.

Mike Deaver was sometimes accused of being an expert at media manipulation. It is my guess that whoever alleged that harbored a good deal of envy for his talent, as well. There is no question that Deaver made the contemporary concept of "photo op" into an art form to achieve the rewards of great media coverage, whether "spontaneously" manipulated or otherwise.

Deaver became famous as the image-maker for President Ronald Reagan. He was a master at staging visually memorable symbolic events—from the fall of the Berlin Wall to the 40th anniversary commemoration of the invasion at Omaha beach. Deaver's artistry created lasting impressions on millions of us around the world.

Former first lady and friend Nancy Reagan said Deaver's greatest skill "was in arranging what were known as good visuals—televised events or scenes that would leave a powerful symbolic image in people's minds."

Deaver was nearly always behind-the-scenes, advising not only President Reagan but countless other leaders—heads of state to titans of industry—on the value of speaking with a clear voice and wise perspective. He was a leading example of people who have changed the world by knowing how to communicate a message, inspire greatness, and create a lasting great impression.

His secret for great communications was to help a leader develop an ability to translate the most complex issue into just a couple of clear sentences using simple words that would lead to positive change. In other words, leaders should take a moment to step back from all the chaos, look at the big picture of what needs to be done, and say it—in a few easy to understand words.

After leaving the White House, Deaver took his quiet manner and enormous talent to independent PR agency Edelman Worldwide, where he reshaped the practice of public relations and helped successful organizations around the world become even more successful. There, I learned from him and treasured his friendship.

Just before his passing in August 2007, Deaver was asked by his colleagues at Edelman to describe the few great communicators he had known, including President Reagan and Dan Edelman, founder of Edelman Worldwide. This is what Deaver said:

"They, and a few of us, got into the world of communications when it was a world of print … then radio and TV and now the Internet, e-mails and blogs … and yet their values remain the same today—

- Know who you are

- Be open and transparent

- Be ready for change

"But the world IS CHANGING," Deaver told his colleagues and friends. He quoted an excerpt from a column by Thomas Friedman in the *New York Times*. Friedman had written:

"When everyone has a blog, a MySpace page, or Facebook entry, everyone is a publisher. When everyone has a cell phone with a camera in it, everyone is a paparazzo. When everyone can upload a video on YouTube, everyone is a filmmaker. We're all public figures now. The blogosphere has made the global discussion so much richer—and each of us so much more transparent. In this transparent world, 'how' you live your life and 'how' you conduct your business matters more than ever, because so many people can now see into what you do and tell so many other people about it on their own without any editor."

What was important to Deaver was "how" we differentiate ourselves in a world that has become so exposed and so easily copied. He talked of getting your "hows" right—how you build trust, how you collaborate, how you lead, and how you say you're sorry.

"More people than ever will know about it when you do—or don't," he said.

CHAPTER THREE

NEW OPPORTUNITIES, BIG MONEY, AND OLD PR

Welcome to life in a multimedia world, an environment that is constantly changing, taking new shape, and then reinventing itself all over again. It is a world in which, for journalists, every minute can be a deadline. It is a world in which what you say in Chicago can be reported almost instantly in London, Singapore, and everywhere in between via new technologies on the Internet, wire services, online streaming video, blogs, and satellite television news.

We are living in a world of such exposure, openness, and transparency that it almost seems we live under microscope slides. There is no such thing as secrets anymore.

This is a world in which the diverse and ever-changing dynamics of new information about current events from countless sources compete for the media's attention. It's a world where a faceless blogger can learn or concoct something hostile about your organization, post it on the Web, and ruin your whole day.

We are in a world in which the news media you knew last year isn't the same media you need to know today and most likely will evolve into something different and even more challenging next year.

In today's highly competitive world, a good news story positions you as a leader, as someone special. A news story about your organization isn't just a heady drug for the ego. Having the media write about your organization builds *your* reputation and enhances *your* brand. It drives awareness and interest in your organization more quickly than anything else. Media coverage opens doors to audiences that might otherwise remain out of reach. Media coverage can make and break legends. A good story in the media can right a wrong.

Yet for many individuals, businesses, and organizations that aim to reach wide audiences, effective media communications remains all too elusive. In the last couple of decades, the value of media relations has been recognized as an influential and solid brand building and marketing tool. Media coverage delivers desired results.

Corporations spend millions on public relations efforts, trying to win favorable positioning in their respective marketplaces by using the awesome reach of the news media, which is a powerful conduit to the public. Still, many organizations feel shortchanged.

Often lacking the expertise in-house, even within their own corporate communications departments, organizations hire public relations agencies in an attempt to achieve prominent media coverage. However, many agencies themselves lack meaningful skills, contacts, and know-how. It is no secret that PR agencies do not, as a general rule, invest in adequate staff training to build competence at strategic communications, writing, or other client service skills.

Why? To find the answer, one must look behind the veil of ownership of many agencies today. Public relations agencies used to be independently owned and many reflected a distinctive regional or national savviness. Clients benefited from the competitiveness, internal pride, and cross-discipline teamwork that came from independence. That's no longer always the case for many agencies, especially the larger or specialized ones.

In recent years, massive financially driven, publicly traded advertising conglomerates have been gobbling up formerly independent public relations, advertising, and marketing firms, including most major agencies.

Omnicom Group now owns Fleishman-Hillard, Porter Novelli, and Cone and Ketchum, to name just a few of its hundreds of holdings. WPP owns Burson-Marsteller, Hill and Knowlton, GCI Group, and Ogilvy among its galaxy of PR and advertising firms. French giant Publicis Groupe owns Manning Selvage & Lee Public Relations, headquartered in New York. And, on the list goes.

These enormous multi-national conglomerates, many based in

Europe, own hundreds of public relations, marketing, public affairs, branding, and advertising agencies. The holding companies view agencies as moneymaking machines, and the demand big payoffs. In this world of conglomerates, high billable hours and tight-fisted control of budgets equal ever-increasing profits.

Incidentally, you may seek a public relations agency and consider four agencies that are all owned by the same multi-national advertising holding company, only to have a couple drop out for conflict-of-interest reasons because they represent your competitors. However, when you select another agency, the ultimate beneficiary of profits from your account may be the same holding company that owns the agencies that originally dropped out of the bidding.

The agency holding company concept is brilliant for investors but causes an obsession with making as much money from clients as possible while keeping overhead low. For agency managers, it is often an untenable situation—make your numbers or else. The "or else" part means the manager may not get a bonus or promotion or, in the worst case, may lose his or her job completely. Needless to say, staff training has taken a backseat to numbers.

In an environment in which employees are expected to bill at least seven and one-half hours each work day to client work, internal training programs at even the largest PR agencies are woefully lacking or do not exist; professional education to build or improve skills pulls agency personnel away from client billable hours.

The emphasis on billable time is similar to that of law firms. However, the big difference is that lawyers graduate from law school better trained when they initially get hired than most young graduates who join PR shops without any practical experience.

Within the public relations industry, agency veterans are beginning to criticize the lack of training as being incredibly shortsighted and thus leading to the possibility of shallow work for clients.

Doug Poretz of the independently owned Qorvis Communications in Washington believes the fundamental model of most public relations agencies is "broken and outmoded." Poretz maintains that the only thing today's clients want are value and results, yet most agencies sell time, what he calls "an outdated commodity."

There is a clear and obvious disconnect, according to Poretz.

PR service providers are selling something the customers don't want. He also maintains that the hourly billing model is to blame for high employee and client turnover at many public relations agencies.

Qorvis is a relatively new agency and has grown rapidly on the PR scene, partly because it snagged a multi-million dollar account: the attempt to polish the image of Saudi Arabia in the wake of the September 11, 2001 terrorist attacks.

Qorvis' business model is likely to succeed; the future of its client relationships is based on performance and measurable results rather than billable hours.

The head of corporate communications for a leading Fortune 500 corporation, who asked to remain anonymous, agrees that today's PR agency model is broken and obsolete.

"Too often," he said, "they want to counsel and strategize rather than be accountable for action and results."

He went on to share that many of the top PR agencies use a standard format to handle a client's brand, reputation, or media challenge. Regardless of the industry or uniqueness of the client or situation, the agencies use the same approach with little or no customization.

The fate of even a multi-billion dollar organization's brand and public reputation is often placed in the hands of junior level, lower-paid, and sometimes ill-prepared PR agency staff. These inexperienced staff members are charged with figuring out how to communicate your news and gain publicity without messing things up. Guess who gets blamed and canned first when PR programs crash and burn?

You may wonder whether public relations agencies really care to accomplish good results on your behalf and at your expense. The answer is often, yes. But far too many agencies, especially the big, multi-national firms, care more about getting their hands on your fat budget than on your reputation and message.

To ensure that a PR agency is focused on results, my unnamed acquaintance at the Fortune 500 corporation suggests that you ask your PR agency these overly candid questions and measure their responses:

- What skill set do you value most in your people? Writing skills, humility, and outside agency experience are all good and extremely rare answers.

- How do you incentivize your people through base and variable compensation? Run away, he said, if growth is mentioned before customer satisfaction.

- What metrics do you use to measure customer satisfaction? Look for a clear answer that indicates, for example, customer surveys or increased favorable press. If the agency people awkwardly measure their words or look at each other in search of an answer, walk away.

- Will you contract on a pay for performance basis? The best agencies will at least consider this option, as it ties their performance to your organization. Watch their expressions when you ask this question.

These are challenging yet fair questions. Within today's context of the big agency model, such questions are completely appropriate. Agency margins are under pressure from holding companies, and when agencies hire and fire staff as they win and lose clients, they find it difficult to attract and keep the best talent. You want to be sure that skilled employees are attracted to—and maintained on—your account.

Some of the most-recognized names in the public relations industry have self-serving business models that focus on making money to keep the holding company beast happy. Such agencies are experts more at getting your business rather than keeping it. PR insiders call the practice "churn and burn." Agency leaders generate as much new business as possible and then immediately hand it off to lower-paid staff who are billed out at embarrassingly high rates despite their junior level of expertise. The agency assumes that clients will hang with them for at least a year; there is a grace period that allows for mistakes. By the time a client finally fires the agency for poor performance, agency leaders have snagged newer clients.

CHAPTER FOUR

SURROUND YOURSELF WITH TALENT

As a leader of a business or organization, how can you find a smart communications strategist and/or a savvy public relations agency that really "gets it" and delivers the results you expect?

After interviewing leaders of companies, associations, and not-for-profit organizations, I repeatedly heard four general warning signs that may help you identify ineffective agencies or strategists:

- Too lopsided a budget versus work discussion. If an agency seems more interested in the size of your budget than in your expectations for hiring an agency, beware.

- Too many expensive suits in the room. If an agency has too many senior level people in the room, beware. Let's get real ... they show up for window dressing. Don't count on them to do much work on your account.

- Too much talk, too little listening. If agency representatives talk too much about how great their agency is while not listening to your needs, beware.

- Too much arrogance. If an agency seems too full of its ego, beware. Too much ego can suggest too little competence.

I will address additional warning signs later in this chapter. It is important to take a look behind the curtains—the smoke and mirrors—for a reality check about today's public relations industry. What you find may help you decide whether you need an outside agency or more expertise in-house.

In public relations today, clients recognize the need for image management in addition to the marketing value of effective, favorable, and accurate media coverage. Often lacking the skills among in-house staff, businesses turn to PR agencies for help and support. Yet, in the area of strategic communications—achieving earned media coverage for clients—some agency managers tend to minimize the value of media relations skills with a dismissive air that suggests, *anyone can call reporters, I prefer to do more lofty and important things ...*

The shocking truth is that many agency managers never learn or fail to keep up-to-date with the practical and evolving skills of strategic communications. While such managers might talk a good line with clients, many do not know how to develop a top-level communications strategy in today's hotly competitive news media environment. As a result, they hand off the responsibility to junior agency staff to, well, sink or swim.

Washington public relations agencies, for example, are full of senior level executives who were former presidential appointees for various federal government agencies. Their backgrounds typically include working as a functionary on a campaign or being the spouse of a major contributor. The payback—generally after considerable lobbying—is appointment to the public affairs department of federal agency, often because they lacked skills for other departments.

After a year or two with the government, they go to work for a PR agency where they most likely will be marketed as a so-called top expert in the fields of energy, healthcare, transportation, security, technology, or whatever. During new business presentations, it's common for agencies to boast—in terms of near-mystical gravitas— that these former *presidential appointees* can just pick up the telephone and have immediate access to top people within the government to make things happen. Often, the truth is stretched. "Big hat, no cattle," as the saying goes.

Investigative reporter Ken Silverstein of *Harper's* magazine went undercover in 2007 to expose the extent to which a Washington, D.C., public relations firm would go to land a lucrative account. The goal was to improve the image of and to win friends in the nation's capital for the notoriously repressive and dictatorial government of Turkmenistan.

Silverstein's exposé, which questioned the ethical boundaries and money lust of a PR agency, not only made the cover of *Harper's,* but was reported widely by mainstream newspapers, including the *Washington Post,* and numerous blogs. Even the PR firm that was the target of Silverstein's article—APCO Worldwide—perpetuated media awareness by posting an ad hominem attack on Silverstein that appeared on the agency's Web site for all to see and even included links to other media coverage.

Soon after, there was a series of spoofs in the popular cartoon strip Doonesbury by Garry Trudeau featuring two Martini-imbibing, sunglasses-wearing PR pros discussing how to solve the image problems of Greater Berzerkistan, a fictional country in which the President-For-Life's ethnic cleansing practices represent a big challenge—"That pig's gonna need a lot of lipstick," one of strips said. The PR people in Doonesbury go on to discuss having a golf tournament and a jingle— "something bluesy, perhaps, to go with genocide." The cartoon strip, which mirrored the tone of the *Harper's* exposé, appeared in hundreds of newspapers.

Over a period of ten weeks, I asked APCO Worldwide to voice their side of the story that appeared in *Harper's,* but they did not make anyone available.

Silverstein's exposé underscored the no-holds-barred atmosphere among PR firms. Some have been known to win significant international accounts, and then assign account people who lack international experience, do not have passports, and have never traveled or worked abroad.

While consulting and lecturing on today's latest trends in communications to help enhance the competitive positioning of corporations in Slovenia and Croatia, I met the founder of the London School of Public Relations, John Dalton. This is the back-story he proudly shared with me about how his school started and has grown.

The London School of Public Relations (LSPA) has become a kind of phenomena, primarily in the CEE—Central and Eastern Europe—countries that are working to establish their own niche in today's exciting new Europe.

Over the years, Dalton, a failed accountant by his own admission and with no public relations credentials, has been teaching public relations people at small agencies in Eastern Europe. The PR agencies pay Dalton to license the London School of Public Relations name. He works then with these agencies to attract new clients through the caché of a prestigious-sounding institution.

The London School of Public Relations, incidentally, has no association, endorsement, or relationship with the respected London School of Economics.

Dalton unapologetically states that clients simply are impressed with the name of his outfit. Yet, he also expresses disappointment that the LSPR concept has not successfully attracted attention in Western Europe and the United States. I believe that in more competitive and sophisticated markets, clients expect more than just a name—they expect greater expertise, credentials, and accomplishments.

Yet, even in the U.S., agencies often fail to deliver, especially in the area of meaningful media exposure for clients. Part of the reason is that few people who are assigned to communicate or deal with journalists have the experience it takes in today's media world. Even many so-called media relations experts who regularly counsel clients sadly lack deep experience; most have never worked a day in a newsroom.

Perhaps more troubling is that many agencies have not kept pace with developments in today's digital and online revolution. While they might talk about blogs, they don't necessarily know that blogs are quickly giving way to new methods for communications, such as online data management systems, open source ecology, and RSS newsfeeds, just to name a few. These fresh approaches are opening up a new spectrum of interactive tools to reach and communicate with audiences.

So many people in the public relations industry are so out of touch with today's media communications realities that they actually could put a client's brand and corporate reputation at competitive risk.

Managing a client's reputation and brand image through a strategy of earned media—publicity generated through editorial influence as opposed to paid advertising—can be accomplished with adequate training. But the reality is training rarely happens within PR agencies. Consequently, junior staff members who are assigned the task of getting media coverage for clients use telephone directory-sized volumes of media contact reference catalogs; the catalogs are sorted by news beats, publications, cities, and so on. Although some of the contacts listed are still valid by the time the catalogs are printed, many are not.

It is only common sense that someone who has worked in news media would know how journalists think, what they are looking for, and what is needed for a reporter to make a *story*; a reporter does not need public relations hype.

To successfully communicate your message through the digital revolution of New Media, agency staff assigned to your account should have practical, personal experience in New Media. And unfortunately, this is rarely the case in the PR agency world today, regardless of agency size.

Agency representatives may use jargon or buzzwords that are particular to the business they are pitching, even if they use the words incorrectly. For example, not too long ago, a technology company held a briefing session with several prospective PR agencies as the company considered whether to hire an agency. When it was finally his turn to speak, the president of a leading PR agency repeatedly used the word "algorithm." Each time he said "algorithm," he used the word incorrectly. He even attempted to use "algorithm" as a verb.

This agency president went on to throw out names of top journalists as if they were his blood brothers; he seemed to be guaranteeing fabulous stories for the prospective client. He suggested that reporters would deliver great media coverage from him for merely the price of lunch at a good restaurant. Despite his boasts, this simply isn't the way good media coverage works in today's world.

"The 'old days,' when PR pros went largely unsupervised as they built press relationships via lunches, dinners, and other forms of contact, appear to be over," observes Jack O'Dwyer. He should know. O'Dwyer has been reporting on the public relations industry in his O'Dwyer publications for four decades.

"PR has become a much more disciplined field where agency people usually keep track of how they spend each hour of the day," he says.

"Propelling this discipline is the fact that the great majority of the 15 biggest PR firms have been acquired by the large advertising agency holding (or financial investment) companies. Management and financial controls have become standard in a field once known for its looseness. Worldwide accounts in the multi-million dollar category demand such controls if PR firms are to keep control of their costs."

Yet, issues of quick profits and return on investment aside, does this business model reflect old-fashioned thinking at the expense of expanding the PR industry's expertise into a New Media world? Or, does it suggest a scramble for a fast buck?

Part of the answer is seen in the healthy, solid growth of truly independent and smaller agencies.

Revenue at Qorvis Communications, which I have already mentioned, and Edelman Worldwide, the largest independent global agency, has soared due to their focus on delivering results through intelligent plans, emphasizing openness and transparency, and requiring accountability. Many independent agencies report annual growth rates of 11 to more than 30 percent, which suggests that an increasing number of clients prefer better results and more personalized support from independently owned public relations agencies than from the traditional industry giants.

As head of global communications for Gulfstream Aerospace, a worldwide corporation and client of a major international public relations agency (which I inherited when I took the job), I found that although the PR agency had offices in far-flung world capitals, each office was its own profit center and, consequently, operated in silos. Each office coveted its own business. Communications among offices was cautious to the point of being secretive for fear of losing business to another office within the same agency. When Gulfstream needed support services from several of the agency's offices, the hourly billing rates were shocking. I had the impression that each regional office viewed our business as manna from heaven.

Here is an example. When we asked for the agency's offices in Los Angeles, London, and Hong Kong to help at an event by sending two or three people, nearly everyone in the office showed up, including the top managers who were billed at $400 an hour and just stood around. We also discovered—much to our aggravation— that the agency's offices did not share information about our events so we had to brief each office from scratch, which also increased billable hours.

Incidentally, the PR agency seemed to work hardest when attempting to claim credit for our brand-building successes, even though their contribution was insignificant at the time.

During many interviews with corporations, organizations, and PR agencies—in addition to the media—in preparation to write this book, I found that similar performance by even the largest global public relations agencies is fairly commonplace. They might be huge, employ a lot of people, have multiple offices (which is usually accomplished through the purchase of existing agencies), and make tons of money, but they still operate in silos and the level of expertise among offices is inconsistent. It's a sadly dismal yet accurate picture.

On the other hand, such an environment presents tremendous opportunities for the C-level executive who wants to learn how to capture the media spotlight and establish a reputation as a compelling and charismatic leader.

Let's expand that earlier checklist of tips to help you find a public relations agency that can deliver top quality results for your organization:

- Size does not matter. The size of a PR agency today is meaningless and not relevant to quality of work. In fact, there is some belief that today's super-sized global agencies have been grown that large only in order to charge super-sized fees. That may work for large clients with significant budgets that get an ego-thrill by dropping the name of their agency but it does not always equate to meaningful results. What's far more important is solid expertise to specifically deliver solutions that will help you become more successful.

- Reputation within your own business arena. Ask your colleagues, customers and even competitors what PR agency they believe delivers the best results.

- Be sure the agency really understands the business you are in. So many client-agency relationships fail because the agency does not fully understand a client's business or the client has not honestly expressed personal expectations that are more important than stated objectives.

- Big guns often fire blanks. Determine who has the experience, who will do your work, and who will be accountable. PR agencies, especially the big ones, have a business model of presenting the "big guns" during new business presentations and then hand the work off to junior staff once they win your business. On the other hand, a senior level communications sole practitioner with deep credentials, vast contacts, savvy approaches, and a network of similar professionals with complimentary skills might be far more beneficial to create the results you need than a so-called full-service global agency.

- Chemistry. Chemistry with the communications team is important; it will lead to results. I suppose it is not unlike dating. While I researched the factors in finding the right agency match, Barbara Robinson at Dun and Bradstreet said it best, "chemistry between the agency and the internal team … will the agency be fun to work with. PR is hard work so why not make the hard work fun?"

- Gut sense. Rely on your intuition to judge what people say and how they conduct themselves.

- Top quality strategic communications strategists. Partner with people who know competitive trends, take pride in accomplishing terrific results for their clients, and are authentic professionals in their field. Invest in the talent of such professionals and you will enjoy outstanding results. After all, you are entrusting them to successfully enhance the image, reputation, and brand of your organization.

- Strategic communications consultants are not simply vendors. The people who supply your office with computers, IT services, and coffee machines are vendors. Invest in smart communications pros with clever ideas to competitively position your organization and to become even more successful.

Consider a bold new direction. As an executive, continue reading because you will learn everything you need to know about today's media trends. Then, take charge and beef up your own communications team with world-class expertise. Go out and hire some strategic communications pros and former journalists who can enhance your organization's brand and bottom-line.

CHAPTER FIVE

FLUFF IS FOR PILLOWS

Gone are the days of a fluffy PR department in a back office with staff that just writes press releases and takes long lunches. Savvy strategic communications in today's New Media world is more accountable and can achieve impressive results—but only when an organization hires exceptional leaders with deep credentials and then gives them a seat at the decision-making table. Equate what you want accomplished versus what you think it is worth; avoid the temptation to cheap it out.

Do research within your organization to frankly determine the value of your objectives. What is the value of enhancing and protecting your brand and reputation? Look at examples within your own industry and then hire solid communications professionals.

Most of all, when you hire outstanding communicators, be open to the new ideas they bring and ready to consider the changes and improvements they suggest.

Let me share an example of opposites. Apple and Dell both make computers yet Dell's internal PR efforts are more old school while Apple's corporate communications team is the best, in my opinion, of any on the planet, regardless of industry. Dell hires several agencies in hopes of getting PR expertise the company lacks in-house; Apple does not hire outside agencies but rather invests in assembling a staff with extensive skills. Apple's communications team is easily accessible; Dell's is not.

Here's a little test that I actually tried. Let's pretend I was a general assignment reporter at a daily newspaper. My editor asked me to contact both Apple and Dell to ask some questions for a story because the paper's technology reporter was on vacation. I was under a deadline and I had no contacts at either company. My first task would be to check the companies' respective Web sites.

At the bottom of Apple's home page, I clicked Media Info and was taken to a Media Resources page where I found everything I needed—all the names, e-mail addresses, telephone numbers, and areas of responsibility of every Apple corporate communications employee. I found all the contact information and could make a call to the right person at Apple within 30 seconds.

Dell's Web site was another story. I clicked Contact at the bottom of the home page but there was nothing about media contacts. So, I had to go fishing and clicked Site Map. There, I found Press Room but when I clicked on it, there were no references to specific contacts for the news media staff; there was only a generic form that I could fill out. I completed the form but never heard back from anyone at Dell.

Dell has what I would label an old-fashioned PR department; Apple has a media savvy one. Now, I have a question for you: Which kind of communications department does your organization have?

It's not surprising that Apple greatly overshadows Dell when it comes to capturing headlines, publicity buzz, and superb media stories. All the media attention that Apple generates creates what marketing people call "the halo effect," because the payoff is directly seen in higher sales and shareholder value.

When Apple debuts a new laptop, it makes headlines; Dell, however, relies largely on paid advertising and a press release that reads similar to previous ones. Apple's coverage in both today's mainstream and New Media eclipses Dell's efforts, which are quite simply feeble by comparison. Apple's sales, growing market share, and customer satisfaction reflect the success. Within one year—between 2006 and 2007—Apple's computer laptop sales grew more than 20 percent.

There is also little doubt about which company is the more dynamic brand and visionary market leader into the future of technology. Certainly paid advertising helps, but today's most exciting and impactful strategic initiatives are driven by outstanding strategic communications that reach out to connect with all of today's changing forms of what we call "the media."

There is an important trend happening today as more and more organizations recognize the importance and value of clearly communicating vision with greater influence by generating outstanding news media coverage: A growing number of today's most successful organizations are making the investment in beefing up their communications team in-house rather than gambling to hire outside help.

Look closely at the organizations led by Branson, Jobs, Miller-Muro, Gary Shapiro, Oprah, and others, and you will see top-notch communications teams on staff. From the perspective of these leaders, an in-house team knows the workings of their own organizations, the competitive landscape, the authentic story that needs to be communicated, and the visionary leadership of the person at the helm better than any outside agency or consultant. The contacts and relationships they forge with journalists are invaluable.

The payoff benefits to these organizations are significant, ranging from a greatly enhanced level of accountability to delivering brand awareness and excitement to broad and diverse audiences and increased shareholder value. Sounds like a smart investment to me.

CHAPTER SIX

A MATTER OF COMMON SENSE

I find it astonishing when I run across someone who claims to be a so-called interview technique coach who has never worked as a journalist or written a real news story. Believe me, there are a lot of them out there.

When I spoke with Stuart Elliott, who covers the advertising and marketing industries for the *New York Times*, he began by saying that calling a reporter with a story should be "a matter of common sense" but, instead, what he sees on a daily basis is "ignorance."

Ignorance about what the media needs and how the media works is the biggest fault among public relations people who call Elliott with a story pitch. It's easy, he explained, for a PR person to get a feel for the stories and angles he covers for the *Times* through a quick Google search, but PR people don't seem to bother. Elliott may be one of the most outspoken but he is certainly not alone in this complaint.

While listening to his perspective, which mirrors that of many other news people I have interviewed, I couldn't help being struck by the reality that the public relations industry hasn't done a good job—at least in the minds of many news people—of keeping up with the times and changing trends in journalism.

Elliott said he is annoyed by continuous calls from PR people trying to pitch something he doesn't cover or to "fix" bad coverage they've gotten someplace else, like a competing newspaper. Most PR people, he said, are neither aware nor sensitive to his story deadlines for the *Times*. All these issues can be easily resolved through training, he said, but he is not seeing any evidence of improvement. On the contrary, Elliott said he believes it is getting worse.

For decades much of the public relations industry has churned out volumes of press materials in the same old, predictable, and dull fashion. They use junior staff members to call and pitch to as many reporters as possible—also usually in a predictable and dull fashion. That's the approach that aggravates Elliott and other respected journalists.

News people are always looking for interesting stories to report.

What reporters ask is that public relations people comprehend the difference between a story and the PR fluff that wastes their time and then learn how to present the story idea in a professional and timely manner.

Then there is the matter of all the news releases that flood into newsrooms around the country each day—literally, thousands of them.

Corporations and not-for-profit organizations alike still spend days working to draft a single news release, often on some self-serving subject, not mindful of whether what they have to say might be of interest to the media or outside audiences.

I've seen executives get so wrapped up in writing a news release that they lose comprehension of what it is and begin to believe their news release will miraculously capture national headlines. With few exceptions such coverage just doesn't happen. Nonetheless, they draft and rewrite, passing it from executive to attorney and back again. Everyone will initial it. The process can take days. The press release will be filled with glowing quotes about how "thrilled and excited" organization members are about their announcement. And then it's sent out, perhaps on an expensive news distribution service, to a news media that has been bombarded by hundreds of similar news releases that same day. Seldom does anyone in the media really care. The news release that consumed so much time to assemble will just seem to vanish.

Of course the media often is blamed for its bias or for not recognizing the gravitas of the release, but that's not the case at all.

Gary Shapiro, chief executive of the highly respected Consumer Electronics Association, views many press releases as negotiated documents when they are approved by CEOs, lawyers, and even board members. In some companies, a whole group of top-level people are involved in the approval process. Consensus documents, Shapiro contends, are generally not that strong, and who could argue with that?

If there was agreement on one thing among the many journalists I interviewed for this book it was over the fact that news releases—while still a mainstay of traditional public relations—have today become the least effective method for attempting to get the media's attention. The problem is the host of PR outfits that prosper by talking organizations into issuing more releases or simple naivety and outdated thinking about how to get the attention of today's media.

Daily newspapers receive thousands of news releases each day. The PR industry has an old habit of overwhelming the media with such releases, most of which never get a glance in the newsroom.

If you want results in today's media, you need to embrace new approaches and techniques. That's what journalists say. You need to understand the competitive forces of the news business and you need to be focused and relevant.

Today's journalists are under mandates from their editors to report fresh, new, and clever stories that will help to give their news organizations an edge over the competition and create ways to increase revenue—through paid readership, viewer subscriptions, and advertising. Why, then, should any reporter give your news release a second glance when you have sent it to everyone under the sun, including numerous other people within the same newsroom as well as competitors? It simply does not work that way.

You need to get to know a key reporter and give him or her a real story. What's more, your chances for making a story happen increase when you provide reporters with resource material, including concise and relevant background, visual material, spokespersons, and opposing viewpoints for balance.

In gathering material for this book, I listened as countless journalists complain that PR people fail to comprehend what makes for a timely and legitimate news story.

Jean Cochran, longtime news anchor on National Public Radio's "Morning Edition," told me, "When someone has asked me how to get their story on NPR, my answer has always been: Make it news. I'm sorry, but the PR business is anathema to me."

Cochran raises a fundamental difference in focus between professional journalists in the mainstream news media and efforts by many PR people to get their clients before the media. Reporters think in terms of legitimate news stories. Yet many PR people often miss the point in understanding that essential fact, she and other journalists say.

"I work in an ivory tower," she says, "where we base our editorial decisions on news values. PR people are in the business of trying to gain free publicity for their clients. And, that's of no use to me as I go about deciding the stories I'm going to write each hour."

Cochran speaks for many journalists who see a need for healthy communications between organizations and the news media yet wish that PR people would better comprehend what the media needs.

Another reporter for a leading weekly news magazine, who asked that I not use his name, was particularly revealing about his feelings toward public relations versus journalism.

"When my DNA split back in college," he said, "and I proceeded down the journalism evolutionary track, I basically stopped thinking about how PR people do their jobs. I'll admit I come across some who seem to merge their interests with mine better than others. But every time I hear a reporter complaining about how clueless a PR person is, I usually say, 'Yeah, but imagine what it's like to be the flack for (fill in the CEO name here).' I think about that for about a nanosecond and then it's on to the next story. I have enough work just trying to do my own job well."

We live in a highly competitive world filled with smart and busy people fighting for attention to promote a product, a brand, or an agenda. It's in that environment that journalists work. Whether they work in broadcast or print, they are trained and paid to find timely and interesting news and to write interesting stories that not only meet their audience's needs and expectations, but also help to competitively boost the image of their news organizations.

Jennifer Barrett, an associate editor for *Newsweek*, told me, "I know this may sound dry, but honestly the best pitches are those that come from PR people who have done their homework: they've read my stories, they know my beat and interests, and they've tailored their pitches accordingly.

"I have established rapport with a few publicists I really trust.

And when they pitch me a story, I immediately take notice. I am more skeptical of new names.

"And, it really peeves me," Barrett said, "when publicists with whom I don't have a working relationship use slang or the type of language that my friends would use in personal e-mails—like emoticons (☺) and 'What's up?'—or when a PR person I don't know (and who has not explained to me who his or her clients are) asks, 'What are you working on?' I know that sounds kind of harsh, but rather than ask that question, it would be helpful if PR people just sent me a list of their clients and a list of topics on which they could comment."

Barrett's message is clear: She prefers to work with trusted sources and media relations people who demonstrate a high level of professional skill and competence. She seeks only legitimate stories … and those that don't waste her time with trivia.

While researching this book, I heard Barrett's sentiments again and again as I talked with journalists. Her perspective is echoed by Lisa Mullins, the anchor and senior producer of "The World," an international news program produced by BBC News and heard on public radio stations across America. "It usually takes a nanosecond to determine whether a publicist knows our program, anticipates what sparks our interest, and even believes in what he or she is pitching," Mullins said. "All of these things affect a PR person's credibility. And once that credibility is gone, it's hard to get it back. Honesty is hugely important. I want to be able to trust your pitch."

Marcus Chan, a technology editor at the *San Francisco Chronicle*, told me that he is amazed at how often PR people don't do their basic homework.

"I'm often pitched on topics or products," he said, "that—had the PR person researched our coverage—would know that they were of little interest to us. I'm also amazed by PR folks who leave me voice mails asking which reporter covers a particular industry."

Sometimes—in fact more often than not—a story needs an unusual twist to cut through competitive clutter and get the media's attention. My colleagues in the public relations industry might call it *spin*, but that word lost some credibility in recent years, as too often spin is associated with trying to make a topic legitimate when it's not. When you employ an unusual twist, on the other hand, you use your imagination to come up with a clever new way to present a real, honest-to-goodness story to the media.

Let me share an example. In a tough competitive bid against a major entertainment publicity firm in Los Angeles, the agency I founded and led won the account to launch the new image of a still relatively unknown community called Branson, Missouri. Branson is a place where many respected senior citizen stars of the country music world have settled and continue to perform.

Andy Williams has his Moon River Theater there. The Presley family (no relation to the King of Rock 'n' Roll) has their Country Jubilee Theater. Ray Stevens has his own theater, and so does the popular country music violinist Shoji Tabuchi. More than 30 luxurious music halls have been built in Branson in the last 15 years.

No one seems to know why this started or why so many country music performers were attracted to Branson, but the theaters are filled with fans every afternoon and evening and the shows are terrific. Perhaps Branson is best chalked up as a middle-class American phenomenon.

When my strategic communications agency began working with Branson, awareness of the town was limited to a few surrounding states. Attendance at its shows was an already impressive 1.3 million a year. But local entertainment leaders had a bigger dream.

Theater owners had formed an association, the Ozark Marketing Council, which was our client. They had two goals: achieve national awareness for Branson and push up the annual number of visitors to 3.5 million within two years. They wanted to meet those goals solely through strategic communications.

Clearly an entertainment publicity angle focusing on the individual country music stars could not meet those goals. That approach, while fairly logical, just could not reach and excite the sheer number of people that Branson needed, because the approach would be limited largely to the entertainment media.

Our plan was to capitalize on Branson's allure of being relatively unknown—something new and trendy. A little research showed that Branson had already eclipsed Nashville in annual visitors and was starting to get into the league of places like Disney World. So we planned a "grand opening" of Branson's new season of stars and the pitch to the national news media went something like this:

"Let me tell you about a place you have never heard of. It's called Branson, Missouri. It's in the Ozarks of southern Missouri and only reachable by two-lane mountain blacktop. But last year Branson attracted nearly one-third the total number of tourists of Disney World. And yet you have never heard of the place. Right?" We always stopped there to let those impressive nuggets of information sink in and get a reaction.

Then we continued, "The tourists are there because nearly every country music star you can name—from Andy Williams to the Gatlin Brothers to Mel Tillis—is performing at the dozens of music halls along that two-lane blacktop. And the biggest season ever starts in three weeks. Everybody will be there ...." By the end of that pitch, we usually had their attention.

Many news decision makers would ask us who else was covering the story. It was a legitimate question, considering the timely nature of our pitch and the competitiveness of the media. At first, when we had no firm commitments, we would answer, "Well, we are getting a lot of interest from so-and-so," and drop the names of their competitors. It was a true claim, because most of the news people we contacted expressed real interest.

We straightforwardly communicated that Branson was expected to be a big story that season, and there would be competition for the story. Within the world of the news business, that translates into, "If we're not there, we'll get scooped by our competitors!"

Then what can only be described as a snowball effect happened. One major news organization confirmed they would come, then another, and another. Soon the momentum was almost beyond our comprehension. I recall calling our client to say that the "CBS Morning Show" wanted to originate live for nearly a week from the Ray Stevens Theater. An hour later, we confirmed the "The Larry King Show."

When The Associated Press ran an advance national story for us about all the excitement building for the upcoming opening of Branson's biggest season ever, things really heated up. Then *TIME* ran a cover story on Branson, and our phones rang constantly with other news organizations wanting to know how to be a part of the action.

For the people who ran Branson, a different kind of snowball was forming. They were getting calls from other country music stars who wanted to join in. Soon people like Willie Nelson, Johnny Cash, Glen

Campbell, and Loretta Lynn were showing up to perform at the town's music halls.

In retrospect, I would describe the event as country music's version of Woodstock, except that in Branson the fans were entertained by a fellow dressed as a hobo named Steamboat Willie, among others, while at Woodstock they heard Richie Havens, Jimi Hendrix, and the performers of another genre.

By the time the season opened, the narrow roads of Branson were filled not only with country music enthusiasts but also with satellite trucks from television networks and stations across the country.

During that two-week grand opening at Branson, we attracted coverage and live broadcasts by the *Today Show*, *CBS Morning Show*, *TIME*, *People*, *Newsweek*, *NBC Evening News*, *CBS Evening News*, *ABC Evening News*, the Associated Press, Reuters, the *New York Times*, the *Larry King Show*, countless local television news remotes from across the country, too many newspapers to count and, of all things, the *Wall Street Journal*, which wrote a glowing editorial about the Branson phenomenon.

One day during the high point of the coverage, we got all the country music stars together for a photo event on a large hilltop meadow in Branson. There were more cameras than at a White House news conference, sending images across the country.

Literally overnight millions of people all across America learned about Branson, and all because of exciting news messages that were communicated to vast audiences through the media.

Incidentally, we never sent out a single news release. Not one. Rather we did our homework to identify the correct reporters and editors—journalists who have covered similar faddish and slightly out-of-the-ordinary events before—and then got on the telephones to pitch them with an appealing story.

Branson's star took off like, well, a shooting star. That season alone, the town attracted more than 3 million visitors. There were traffic jams for days on that now-famous two-lane blacktop. The theaters, theme parks, motels, curio shops, and restaurants were packed—and it hasn't let up since. Branson, Missouri, became a world-famous entertainment Mecca almost overnight, and it all began with a clever twist on a timely and trendy story for the news media.

I think it is important to mention at this point that this success happened at a time just prior to the online revolution, without the benefit of e-mail or Web sites. So, while the tools of communications that we used were not quite as instantaneous as what we have today, we delivered a huge achievement for our client through a clever, timely, and appealing story angle that we pitched directly to the right news decision-makers.

Our approach had focused not on the obvious—the dozens of country music stars performing at Branson—but on a phenomenon that appealed to the national news media. Here was an entertainment center that few decision makers at the major media centers were aware of but was attracting millions of visitors.

Our strategy was to play to the natural curiosity of the news people who decide what is reported. Most of them are in New York and, at the time, most of those folks in New York had never heard of Branson. The phenomenon captured their curiosity.

One of the easiest ways to achieve good media relations seems to be the hardest for public relations people to understand. People in the news business make their living writing stories that appear online, in newspapers, wire services, and magazines, and on television and radio. To do this they need something new or different—a hook, an angle. Learn what they need for a news angle, give them a legitimate story, provide balanced background information, and the news media will be happy. And you will have achieved fantastic results.

CHAPTER SEVEN

MEDIA THAT SAVES LIVES

Leaders of not-for-profit organizations frequently tell me that they struggle to get much-needed attention from the news media even when they think they have a good story to tell. Their communications people send out a news release, sometimes using costly press release distribution services, and nothing happens. Their public relations people make media calls, and they are greeted only by voicemail and no return calls.

All too often, a non-profit organization works against itself when it attempts to get the media's attention with outdated methods. Reporters have told me about unreasonable delays when they contact non-profits and a lack of understanding about what makes for a timely and meaningful story. Materials are sometimes exaggerated, grammatically incorrect, or not factual.

Media coverage is so important to one Washington-based not-for-profit that the organization's board and several major funders established mandated "deliverables" or goals for the communications staff, including issuing a predetermined number of press releases and targeting a specific number of stories to appear in the media.

This is an impossible and dysfunctional scenario. Such arbitrary and naïve objectives cannot be achieved and further underscores that making news for an organization must never be manipulated by a funder, board member, human resources person, or strategic planner.

Pulling off media coverage in the world of not-for-profits is a challenge and the big names—organizations such as the Gates Foundation, Habitat For Humanity, and Amnesty International—seem to get most of the attention. But others capture the spotlight, too, and we see it when leaders take charge and act like leaders.

Let me share the story of one such leader, Layli Miller-Muro, and the organization she founded, the Tahirih Justice Center. Miller-Muro's non-profit achieves top quality media stories that directly benefit the organization.

The Tahirih Justice Center is widely respected for providing pro bono legal assistance on behalf of immigrant and refugee women and girls. The issues are often controversial, such as providing legal assistance to women who are seeking asylum or refugee status, particularly from Africa, Asia, and the Middle East. Some women are escaping torturous situations, such as female genital mutilation, human trafficking, or brutal domestic violence.

The Center was founded in 1997 by Miller-Muro, who is an attorney. During law school, she handled a case that made headlines worldwide and led to a dramatic change in how the United States treats victims of gender-based violence who seek asylum. The case did not go well until it caught the media's interest.

Fauziya Kassindja was a 17 year-old girl who fled Togo in fear of a forced polygamous marriage and a tribal practice known as "female genital mutilation." After arriving in the U.S. and spending more than seventeen months in detention, Ms. Kassindja was granted asylum in 1996 by the United States Board of Immigration Appeals (the highest immigration court) in a decision that opened the door to gender-based persecution as grounds for asylum.

Her case was argued before the immigration judge by Miller-Muro, and from all indications, it looked as if Kassindja's request for asylum would be denied and she would be sent back to Africa.

The outcome changed, both quickly and for the better after her case caught the attention of *New York Times* reporter Celia Dugger. Dugger wrote a lengthy story not only about Kassindja's cry for help, but exposing the abusive practice of female genital mutilation. The story "Woman's Plea Puts Tribal Ritual on Trial" dominated the front page of *The Times* and continued inside for two complete pages. It was huge and life changing for both Kassinda and Miller-Muro.

Publicists began calling Miller-Muro's home the morning the article appeared. Soon after, national media, including *ABC Nightline,*

NBC Dateline, CNN, and on and on, requested interviews. Steven Spielberg, Sally Fields, and Lauren Hutton all called to offer support. Hillary Clinton's office called, too.

Most importantly, there was a call from the office of then-United States Attorney General Janet Reno who suggested that Kassindja's legal team promptly file a re-request for parole on behalf of Kassindja, who was being detained in a prison pending outcome of her case.

Someone needed to sponsor Kassindja upon her release and, scrambling to meet a tight legal deadline, Miller-Muro turned to the leaders of her religion, the National Spiritual Assembly of the Baháʼís of the United States. Sponsorship agreement was reached with a local Baháʼí community after a quick telephone conference call, the papers were filed with the court, and Kassindja soon experienced freedom in her new home country, the United States.

In order to justify the government's reversal of its position, Reno's office issued a press release citing "new developments" that had come to light in the case and the sponsorship by the Baháʼí community.

Times reporter Dugger ended up writing nearly a half dozen stories about the Kassindja case and each time, the tone and news angle of her story both stimulated coverage by other news organizations and influenced what other journalists reported.

"The media attention made it become an important case to the courts and government," Miller-Muro shared with me. Kassindja's request for asylum was almost unanimously granted by a group of judges who heard the case. There was only one dissenting opinion.

The staggering amount of media coverage from the Kassindja case led to a best-selling book, *Do They Hear You When You Cry*, which was co-authored by Kassindja and Miller-Muro and published by Bantam Doubleday. Miller-Muro used her advance and all of her proceeds from the book to launch the Tahirih Justice Center, which is located just outside Washington, D.C., in Falls Church, Virginia. The Justice Center is a legal advocate for a wide range of issues faced by immigrant and refugee women and is sometimes a woman's only non-partisan force for true justice.

Miller-Muro told me that in the beginning, dealing with media interviews was trial by fire and, with no formal training, she relied on instinct. She drew upon public speaking skills that her father had taught her. Aside from that, she relied on her own common sense and focused on communicating the truth with clear messages about what was right for her client.

"I learned how the media worked by watching TV interviews and reading articles to judge what they were looking for and who seemed most effective," she told me. "I began a practice that continues today of preparing one page of one sentence quotes to memorize that reflect points I want to be sure to make during an interview."

Miller-Muro gave me an example of the Justice Center's advocacy work on the issue of "mail order brides." The international marriage broker industry has exploded due to the Internet and, while some decent marriages may come from it, the unfortunate fact is that is has enabled the institution of marriage to be used as a way for predatory abusers to find their next victims. The Tahirih Justice Center has become a national leader on this issue and, while advocating for changes in laws that address the abuse of women through the international marriage broker industry, it has engaged a successful media campaign.

Regarding mail order brides, Miller-Muro said, "The harsh reality is that the international marriage broker industry allows the institution of marriage to be used by violent predatory abusers to find their next victims." Such a line is a strong quotable quote that nearly always ends up in a story and influences an audience's perception.

"The sentence draws upon our sensibilities about the sanctity of marriage," she said. "And, it communicates the need for a law that prevents predators from looking abroad for their next victim." The Justice Center's media strategy on this issue has resulted in wide bi-partisan support, the passage of a landmark piece of legislation regulating the international marriage broker industry, the win of the first lawsuit in the US against an international marriage broker, and the attention of *Newsweek*, the *Washington Post*, *NBC Nightly News*, the *O'Reilly Factor* on Fox News, and the *Tyra Banks Show*.

In the intervening years since the Kassindja case, Miller-Muro's voice—and that of others at the Center—has been heard as the non-partisan force for true justice countless times in the media, speaking out in support of women's issues.

The Justice Center's emphasis is on focused messages or talking points for what they want to communicate to influence an outcome. At the Justice Center, an interview's objective often is to influence judges, lawyers, lawmakers, members of congress, and academics regarding legislation or court cases.

"Our preparation as an organization," she shared with me, "is to make sure we are all on the same page with the same talking points. We draft a three to five page document of main points we would like to make with supporting arguments and statistics. From that document, we distill our talking points into a one-pager of five to ten sentences to deliver in an interview."

The Justice Center sends out periodic news releases on issues or developments, like a court decision or new legislation, but never expects a press release to result in a news story.

"Press releases are just a way to nudge a reporter to remind him or her that you are here and available to educate them on an issue," Miller-Muro said. "They see us as experts.

"We have never had success using press releases to generate media. It is just a way to keep them up-to-date on issues."

The Justice Center found the practice of blasting out press releases indiscriminately to countless reporters to be "completely ineffective," preferring instead to actively maintain a list of approximately 200 reporters who have expressed an interest in the organization or who write on their issues.

"I will call a few trusted reporters who have accurately reported on us to seek their advice on an issue or to share ideas," she said.

"The truth is that the *New York Times*, Associated Press, and Reuters are the most powerful combination of media in the U.S. because their stories immediately appear in over 400 other newspapers and TV media typically pick up stories from papers."

While Miller-Muro appreciates the power of television news to reach broad and general audiences, the impact does not last very long and does not always achieve the center's objectives. Print coverage, on the other hand, conveys greater credibility and lasts longer because it is archived by the large information databases, including LexisNexis.

When Miller-Muro or the Justice Center makes news, they find that print media is most powerful because people can cite it and quote it as an authority. Print media is far more influential in the field of human rights advocacy. Conversely, the general public has little direct influence on a court decision or piece of legislation.

To this day, the Tahirih Justice Center has never hired a public relations agency but prefers to work on a personal and pro bono level with a few communications consultants who believe in the work of the Center and who willingly give their expertise for developing talking points or sharing media connections.

Long ago, Miller-Muro accepted responsibility for guiding the brand reputation of the Tahirih Justice Center and, in the process, developed a personal style to achieve consistent, meaningful coverage. You can benefit by following Miller-Muro's formula:

- Treat news releases only as a way to maintain awareness from reporters. Never expect a story to result from sending a release.

- Focus on a few journalists with whom you have a relationship to pitch stories to or to ask for advice, avoiding mass outreach.

- Give reporters timely and relevant legitimate stories angles, with personal stories that illustrate your point.

- Craft a page of five to ten sentences—talking points or messages—that you want to say in an interview before ever speaking with a reporter.

- Develop healthy and respectful working relationships with journalists, which means being immediately responsive to their calls, respectful of their deadlines, and corresponding in a professional manner.

- Readily admit when you are not an expert on an issue and refer journalists to other sources who are.

- Before speaking to a reporter, look up their past coverage and understand their likely biases before talking to them.

- Ask the journalist to use the name of your organization when quoting you so that your comments are best put into context.

The responsibility for developing and guiding the Center's media strategy is always handled personally by Miller-Muro and her staff. That level of ownership and accountability is clearly one reason for the organization's enduring record of achieving important and sometimes life-changing media coverage, and it has put Layli Miller-Muro into that exclusive group of leaders who are among the world's most important communicators. Following her method can help you become a world-class communicator, as well.

LEADERSHIP AND THE DIGITAL REVOLUTION

Billionaire entrepreneur Mark Cuban makes it clear about the importance of knowing how to use the Internet to communicate, to engage in conversations with audiences, and to build brand awareness and value. Cuban, as I mentioned earlier, is owner of HDNet, the high definition cable television network, and the Dallas Mavericks, among other ventures.

The Internet has been an essential communication tool for Cuban's business empire. As a high-profile executive, he's actively online and in touch through his personal blog, BlogMaverick.com.

"In the Internet age," Cuban told me, "executives have to learn how to shape information about themselves and their companies, or the Internet will do it for them, and it won't be pretty."

The once-effective support structure for executives and leaders—such as public relations, marketing, and advertising agencies—has been shockingly slow to learn the new and ever-changing trends of how to use the Internet. Conventional methods of getting an organization's messages communicated through the media are either broken or less effective.

It is up to an executive or leader, according to Cuban, to take the initiative and responsibility to get savvy about the Internet, and the new ways of communicating in today's online world at a time when there is chaos within the mainstream media.

It's being said within the news industry that the traditional media gatekeepers—publishers, editors, producers, and other people who decided what is or is not *news*—no longer have any gates to keep. Perhaps the situation is not quite that stark, but the industry clearly is headed in that direction. The news business is undergoing a major evolution, driven by a massive slump in profits at news organizations, shifts in advertising dollars, changes in consumer interests, and new forms of engaging audiences online. The evolving online technology is attracting larger and younger audiences, and not many of them are interested in media tradition.

Mainstream media gatekeepers, particularly at newspapers, are desperate to find what might appeal to today's audiences.

Polls show that younger people, ages 18 to 35, will only occasionally read a newspaper, preferring instead to get their news—or at least the news they care about—from friends, free online sources or by reading *The Onion* (TheOnion.com), or watching the *Daily Show*'s Jon Stewart on the Comedy Central cable network. Those same polls show declining trust in the news media. In response to these and other signals, the mainstream news industry is moving and shifting to stay vibrant.

To appeal to people who once had the time to read newspapers or sit down to watch network newscasts and who are now exploring online social networks, like Facebook, we are seeing new attempts by news organizations to reach audiences. One such effort is through the emergence of *participatory journalism.*

Participatory journalism is a slippery creature because many people seem to know what it should be, but no one has a really good definition of what it really is. Perhaps that is because the concept is new and evolving. The digital revolution has spawned many of these amorphic and curious concepts. So, if you run a business or an organization and someone suggests using a form of participatory journalism to engage your stakeholders, approach it with a measure of caution—when you ask people for feedback, you might not always like what you hear.

Sometimes called "citizen journalism," participatory journalism is breaking down the barriers between traditional news organizations and ordinary folks like you and me who have something to say. Citizen or participatory journalism is opening new opportunities for us to express our voices. Blogs are a good example, and so are the reader comment-email-share features you find associated with stories on the Web sites of many news organizations.

Within your own organization, if someone thinks that a company blog will make you look cool, think again. Managing and maintaining a blog not only consumes significant time and energy in order to be relevant, blogs only function well as a transparent and active exchange or interaction of news, information, and opinions. That means you will not get away with posting something every week or month or it will lose its timely benefit for communicating news. Posting something on a blog also is no guarantee that you will not ruffle someone's feathers and hear about it.

For the media, however, this shift is part of what is being called a democratization of the media, and it seems to be working fairly well. The news business and methods for communicating with today's journalists are changing before our eyes. There are a multitude of new sources today to find the information and news we desire as individuals—sources that were never imagined just a few years ago. The traditional mainstream news industry is being forced to get more in tune with audience desires.

Beleaguered big city daily newspapers, which have been bleeding paid readership and advertising revenue, are combining clever ideas with solid professional reporting in attempts to lure readers. One way is the *conceptional scoop.*

Conceptional scoops are those attention-getting "Wow, I didn't know that!" stories that we cannot wait to share with our friends. They often come about when a reporter re-examines facts that have already been made public and finds an innovative or unusual way of seeing what's behind the facts or the true situation behind the claims—sort of a look at truth and reality behind all the smoke and mirrors in some cases.

Here is an example. Even though President George W. Bush praised laws passed by Congress when he signed them, the *Boston Globe* dug deeper and discovered that the Bush White House had quietly taken the position that the president has the right to ignore the bills he's just signed. In a conceptional scoop, the *Globe* reported that Bush had ignored many of the laws he signed. In fact, the paper reported that he ignored the laws more than 750 times. It was big news and a story covered by other media with credit to the *Globe.*

Phil Bennett, managing editor at the *Washington Post*, sees the conceptional scoop as another form of competitive journalism.

"People who can arrive first at the defining nature of a conceptional scoop—of telling you, 'Here's what these sets of facts mean'—oftentimes control the agenda of the discussion of that subject," Bennett says.

Reporter Jennifer Lee of the *New York Times* defines it more simply as, "stories that people talk about" with their friends.

The *Wall Street Journal* has turned conceptional scoops into solid benefits. They have seen benefits ranging from increased publicity and readership to winning a Pulitzer Prize.

For those in public relations, and for anyone else who works with the news media, it is important to track and understand this 21st century evolution of the media, which is likely to continue for years. The traditional methods of reaching out to the media are obsolete and ineffective. If you want to get the media's attention, strategic communications professionals must adapt savvy and contemporary approaches that fit the media's styles. The challenge today is that no two styles can be precisely the same. As the old cliché goes, the only thing constant about the media today is change.

National Public Radio's Juan Williams summed it up best when he told me, "We live in times of national discontent and tremendous change—political, among demographics, and within our society."

Within that environment, he said, the media is struggling to reinvent itself, connect with audiences, and give their audiences what they want and expect to hear.

During strategic communications workshops and lectures, I have been asked questions about new trends and challenges in working with an ever-changing news media. What works and what no longer is effective? How do I communicate with reporters and bloggers? What is the definition of "journalist" in today's world of amateur online and citizen reporters? How beneficial is online technology for strategic communications—like interactive sites, streaming video, viral word-of-mouth tactics, social networks, Web site newsrooms, and blogs—and what are just the passing fads? What new tools of strategic communications are viable? What's the future of video news releases? How about the effectiveness of traditional media kits, news conferences, and news releases?

Like a modern day gold rush, the public relations industry is scrambling to embrace the elements of online New Media. "Wake up to New Media or Lose Clients," scream the trade headlines.

In the last few years, the hysteria has felt like … well, it's reminiscent of the 1990s when the public relations industry discovered the Internet and e-mail as a way to bombard journalists with unsolicited materials and, before then, when they figured out how a fax machine could inundate reporters with press releases that went unread.

Major public relations agencies now hold internal summit conferences to figure out how best to serve their clients in the digital revolution, exposing how seriously the PR industry has fallen behind the learning curve.

"Senior PR people who aren't tech savvy and who would rather read the *New Yorker* will, at a certain point, have to add blogs to their daily news diet," believes *Newsweek* technology editor and blogger N'Gai Croal. "You can't have just your younger, entry-level staff being the ones who understand New Media."

For starters, it's beyond time to wake up because the tools of New Media have been in use for several years already, and many of today's practitioners of New Media are considerably ahead of the PR profession when it comes to savvy ideas.

Consider, for example, that the definitive *Handbook for Bloggers*, written by Julien Pain and Dan Gillmor, has been online and available *for free for several years*. Reading it might have prevented PR tech-rush fiascos, like the fake (or flack) blog, "WalmartingAcrossAmerica," which was conceived by Edelman Worldwide. Incidentally, "WalmartingAcrossAmerica" actually did not generate much audience traffic or attention until exposed by *BusinessWeek* for its subterfuge and dishonesty.

Even though Edelman took some heat for creating "WalmartingAcrossAmerica," at least the agency was learning by venturing into new and somewhat uncharted territory on the Internet.

Many other PR agencies seemingly have yet to discover the Internet's vast potential as a medium for communication, perhaps reflecting the low-tech knowledge levels of their leaders. The CEO of one well-known public relations agency told me recently that she could still barely figure out how to use e-mail.

The public relations industry traditionally has searched for a better and louder bullhorn to get attention on behalf of clients. The elements of New Media, such as blogs and interactive community sites, are simply high-tech bullhorns.

Anybody can get a moment to stand on a box at Speaker's Corner; it's what they say and to whom that really counts and makes a difference. What good is the tactic of a blog if you brush aside the strategic discipline of defining competitive positioning or lack incisive messages that authentically capture an audience's attention?

Don't get me wrong—I don't want to sound old-fashioned—especially because I was an early user of Internet and blog technology. I love online technology. But, in reality, what we are talking about are just tactical tools. Corporate leaders need to look beyond the latest cool online communications technology, and ask, "What's the strategic purpose?"

Maybe now is the time for a reality check—strategic communications in today's fiercely competitive world mandates clever positioning, understanding audience needs, and knowing how to craft timely and meaningful messages that excite people and create results for clients.

Thomas Friedman of the *New York Times* delivered a sober warning recently when he observed that, "technology is dividing us as much as uniting us."

Technology's New Media is being embraced by many in the public relations industry as the latest magic potion solution for clients while insulating us from actually having to interface with journalists—mainstream and New Media—and the real world, in general. PR still needs to learn how to better communicate with the mainstream media on an interpersonal level and not hide behind press releases. PR still needs to learn the difference between pushing fluff and pitching a real story.

Does New Media reach large audiences? Sometimes, in isolated cases, but not always. For every YouTube, SecondLife, Facebook, MySpace, or TalkingPointsMemo.com, there are tens of millions of sites and blogs that no one will ever hear about.

Gary Shapiro, chief executive of the powerful Consumer

Electronics Association, told me that he questions the benefits of CEO blogs as a way of getting attention because CEOs do not read the blogs of other CEOs. He makes a valid point.

One needs to consider the overall realistic goals of a CEO blog or corporate blogging. Business needs to have measurable and achievable goals for every activity they engage in, and that includes investing the time in blogging.

While I am a proponent of corporate blogging, blogs should have the same responsibility as any other Web page on an organization's site—attract and engage visitors, and hopefully convert them to the next step in a relationship.

Blogs are even more credible in the role of engaging and developing interactive conversations with an organization's audiences and customers when employees are given the freedom and job safety to blog about specific areas of their own expertise. It is at that point when customers may start thinking, "Hey, these guys really know their business, and they care about what I have to say!"

I use the words, "freedom and job safety," for a reason. The risk of misstatement, even unintended innuendo, is enormous on a blog. If an organization encourages employees to blog about their personal expertise, and to openly express opinions about the company, then top executives must accept that not everything said may be rosy and perfectly in-step with what corporate leaders hope for the image of their organization.

When employees have complete job security from their bosses to blog, the payoff ultimately will be enhanced corporate credibility and respect among stakeholders. Quite frankly, I believe that employee blogging can be a good way to building online brand awareness by creating word-of-mouth about your organization.

The safety net for CEO blogging, however, is somewhat riskier. Let me explain. Suppose you, as leader of an organization, have started a blog at the urging of the PR and marketing people to better promote your leadership image. And, one day, something really ticks you off. Perhaps a reporter has said something you didn't like and you feel the need to write a few words about it on the blog. Wham! You have instantly given the journalism and blogosphere a fresh new story to report and the headache is only starting for you.

The executive director of a large trade association in Washington, D.C., decided to have a blog that ultimately cost him his job. When he posted a personal rant about a controversial issue facing his organization, his board of directors asked him to step down from his position. His blog got him fired.

Remember, blogs are merely communications tools and must be used with skill and common sense. Furthermore, there are savvier and safer ways to boost your image and that of your organization.

We are still missing the point that in today's intensely competitive world, the core responsibility of strategic communications is to create authentic competitive differentiation—i.e. greater attention—in fresh and imaginative ways that will deliver meaningful and tangible results.

If you are leading an organization, it is far more important to focus on clear and accurate messages to capture an audience's attention and the interest of reporters.

Are we running the risk that technology will make the practice of public relations even more insular? Will all the gadgets of the digital revolution merely act as a crutch so we can avoid talking to each other and the press and target audiences? In our breathless rush to New Media online, are we perpetuating a troubling copycat technology trend in PR?

And most worrisome, is PR hoping that by creating and manipulating its own image of New Media we can ignore our failures for having the legitimate contacts and knowing how to work with the real journalists at the mainstream news media?

The warning signs are already out there. Perhaps the solution is for PR to improve its own skills in the albeit imperfect craft of communications and then to consider which new tactics are appropriate for our clients and which are not. There are still many agencies practicing a style of PR today that became obsolete years ago.

CHAPTER NINE

JOURNALISM DRIVEN BY PROFITS AND FEAR

With the exception of the PBS *NewsHour* with Jim Lehrer, National Public Radio, news programs on HDNet Television, the *New York Times,* and a shrinking handful of newspapers—we have squarely entered the era of iNugget News, as one pundit observed, which requires little thought or understanding, and certainly does not nourish our perspective of our country or the world.

If you are leading an organization or are responsible for managing communications and the competitive image of a company, it is vitally important you know the details of what's happening in today's media world. The competition is tougher than ever when you want to communicate news about your organization. To identify opportunities, we need to look inside today's news industry to see the competition we face when we knock on the door and what drives their decisions and thinking.

It is essential that the news you want announced about your organization be timely, relevant, and right to the point. Those who are verbose are ignored and/or not trusted.

Remember what Bob Schieffer of CBS News said: When you have something to say, say it "quickly, directly, and clearly"—even though the media itself sometimes gets so cryptic it becomes laughable.

"Libby Convicted of Lying" proclaimed the headline on CNN. That was the conclusion of a four year criminal investigation into the outing of CIA operative Valerie Plame Wilson and the resulting four week trial that exposed the inner workings of the White House public relations propaganda machine and how the Washington news media permitted itself to be manipulated. I. Lewis "Scooter" Libby, Vice President Dick Cheney's right-hand at the White House, was going to prison after being convicted by a jury on four felony counts. (President George W. Bush subsequently commuted Libby's prison sentence.)

The charges were serious and involved the highest levels of the United States government, untruths, perjury, and obstruction of justice. Yet, it was all distilled for the American people into just four words scrolling across CNN's on-screen news ticker.

As a friend at National Public Radio called it, it was "a news hors d'oeuvre." But CNN's description really wasn't even that. An hors d'oeuvre generally leads to something better and more filling. The information and news manipulation that went on as a result of the Libby affair would leave a bad taste in anyone's mouth. But, those are the times in which we live.

Not to be left out, the *Washington Post* has also joined the brevity bandwagon. The paper is faced with dwindling circulation and ad revenues, fierce competition from online news resources, and the popularity of its own free morning tabloid, *Express*, which is handed out to commuters in the nation's capital.

In a staff memo, *Washington Post* former Executive Editor Leonard Downie, Jr. and Managing Editor Philip Bennett wrote, "We have decided to take a more disciplined approach to story lengths ... every story must earn every inch."

As the traditional mainstream news media struggles for survival in today's digital revolution and the proliferation of online information delivery vehicles, the public is bombarded by an ever-increasing avalanche of messages, much of it generated by the public relations industry, and it's not going to let up.

Yet, think about the potential long-term impact of our brevity. Are we—meaning the people in communications who are responsible for pushing these messages out to the public—actually helping to shorten attention spans in our population?

Influenced by the convergence with New Media and the digital online revolution, the way in which the business called journalism is practiced by news organizations has changed at almost the speed of light in recent years. Journalism once focused on reporting events of interest and happenings that might affect our lives. Now, the primary goal of news is to maximize profits by delivering a form of entertainment.

What's most troubling is that this trend in journalism has opened the door for abuse, manipulation, and deception (as we have seen with phony blogs on behalf of corporations). As Americans work harder and for longer hours, we are taking advantage of what free time they may have though clever and manipulative snippets of faux online news and information.

The mainstream news media is embattled. Attacked by political and societal forces both right and left, rocked by scandals, and challenged by upstart bloggers and the changing landscape of technology, the media has become a focus of controversy and concern. Audiences are in decline and the media's credibility with the public is in shreds. It hasn't always been this way, but there is general agreement that the media's reputation began to deteriorate when conglomerates got into the news business and were interested solely in the bottom line.

These changes in the business of journalism today have a direct impact on the practice of strategic communications and our efforts to work with reporters to generate news stories and coverage.

Newsroom staff cutbacks have rocked many news organizations. The venerable *Washington Post* is a typical example. The paper's number of paid subscribers has declined at a rate of four percent a year. During a March 2006 meeting in the *Post*'s newsroom to explain why 80 news people would be laid off, Executive Editor Leonard Downie told them, "It is obvious that a significant change is taking place in our readership, with a sizable portion of it migrating to the Internet."

The popularity of the Internet has impacted the traditional news business where it hurts most, the bottom line.

An Associated Press headline said it all: "Spending on Internet ads reaches new high for 10th straight quarter; newspapers continue to feel pinch."

The story cited an Interactive Advertising Bureau and PricewaterhouseCoopers study that found Internet ad volume in the first quarter of 2007 totaled $4.9 billion, a 26 percent increase from the same time the year before. Advertisers have been accelerating their online ad spending since 2003, and news organizations around the world are feeling the pinch.

In the Philadelphia metropolitan area, the number of newspaper reporters has fallen from 500 to 220 in the last 20 years, according to the Project for Excellence in Journalism at Columbia University. A few years back, five AM radio stations covered news around the city; now there are two. The project describes it as a "seismic transformation" on the media landscape. While this is the current trend in the media across America, it wasn't always that way.

When I walked into the main newsroom of CBS Network News in New York some years ago, I was a very naive young man from northern Virginia and was eager to begin my career as a television journalist. CBS Network News was a legendary place back then. I worked alongside some of the icons of broadcast news: Walter Cronkite, Dan Rather, Mike Wallace, Dallas Townsend, Morley Safer, and Charles Osgood. I had always wanted to be a broadcast journalist, and there I was, among some of the best, and working for an organization that defined broadcast news excellence. It was one of the most exciting times in my life.

No one back then thought of CBS News as a profit center. It had gotten the moniker "the Tiffany network" because of its focus on quality, both in programming and news. CBS set the example for others to follow. The purpose of CBS News and the other networks was to credibly report the news of the day without being encumbered by an eye on ratings and corporate stock value.

At that time, CBS News had a full staff of seasoned editors and producers who checked the facts and looked over every script before it went on the air. So it was at many of the major networks and papers; we would try to find the facts and write stories as accurately and objectively as humanly possible. The emphasis was on quality and solid journalism. We were expected to report the news. Television news in those days made a profound impact on America. It's not that way today.

TV news today is formula-based to give a specific audience only what they expect to hear. It is entertainment-driven and designed to make money. The more sensational the story or the greater the threat of fear it generates, the larger the potential audience and the higher the advertising rates the news organization can extract.

No one should be surprised then that cable news can provide non-stop coverage about the plight of a celebrity's latest problem with substance abuse but cannot impart perspective on the complexity of violence and war in the Middle East. Broadcast news executives say that Americans—more than any other global audience—generally prefer not to hear about world events because, well, those things are too complicated.

Especially since September 11, 2001, fear and excess sells. That explains the unending emphasis on "Fox News Alerts" in bold red letters on our television screens and similar tactics at other TV news outlets.

"Our history will be what we make it. And if there are any historians about fifty or a hundred years from now, and there should be preserved the kinescopes for one week of all three networks, they will there find recorded in black and white, or in color, evidence of decadence, escapism, and insulation from the realities of the world in which we live."

Sounds like a fairly accurate description of television news today, doesn't it? Edward R. Murrow, the legendary CBS newscaster, spoke those words in October 1958.

"Evidence of decadence, escapism, and insulation from the realities of the world ..." I guess television news hasn't come too far. In fact, journalists from every corner of the news industry have expressed concern to me over whether the journalism profession has lost its compass and is going in a circle rather than improving and moving forward.

Murrow went on to say, "I am frightened by the imbalance, the constant striving to reach the largest possible audience for everything; by the absence of a sustained study of the state of the nation."

Over the last 20 years, many once-respected news operations have dramatically cut back on news staffs and quality has suffered.

About the state of television news today, CBS newsman Dan Rather told an audience at Fordham University that there is a climate of fear running through newsrooms stronger than he has ever seen in his more than four-decade career. Politicians of "every persuasion," he said, "have gotten better at applying pressure on the conglomerates that own the broadcast networks" in their attempt to influence news.

Rather called it a "new journalism order." He believes that the advent of the 24-hour cable news competition has led to "dumbed-down, tarted-up" coverage in a desperate chase for ratings. "All of this creates a bigger atmosphere of fear in newsrooms," Rather said.

Reporters are cautious, Rather suggested, about covering stories that might be too controversial or might offend an influential group and, consequently, jeopardize the journalist's livelihood.

Former CNN president Walter Isaacson said, "One of the great pressures we're facing in journalism now is, it's a lot cheaper to hire thumb-suckers and pundits and have talk shows on the air than actually have bureaus and reporters."

In recent years, the major television networks have whittled down the size of their news operations, including closing news bureaus around the world. CBS News has shut nearly all bureaus except Washington and London. What this means is that the networks now rely on freelance reporters and interns who will work for low wages, and video from sometimes less-than-reliable sources.

The trend in television news is *talking head* journalism. It saves money in production and staffing expenses while more efficiently retaining advertising profits.

Rather said, "The substitute for reporters far too often has become 'Let's ring up an expert.' This is journalism on the cheap, if it's journalism at all."

Aaron Brown, the former CNN anchorman, has contended that, "truth no longer matters" in the push by 24-hour cable television news channels to build audience ratings. America has become such a polarized society of the left and the right, he said, that many people are not interested in the truth as much as news that conforms to their viewpoints and entertains them.

Once an altruistic and perhaps too idealistic profession with keen focus on balance, accuracy, and integrity, journalism today is driven by corporate profits—money. Big media conglomerates discovered in the 1980s that news, like entertainment, could be a money machine. The higher their ratings in radio and television news, the more they could demand from advertisers. The bigger the headlines in print, the bigger the flow of ad dollars.

Consequently, news today is presented less to inform and more to titillate, seduce, and entertain. All this has happened at a time when news audiences are being pulled away from traditional news outlets by cable television and Internet news sources.

Television news, for example, has become not so much about

providing depth of understanding for a story as about entertainment and drama. Television reporters are also expected to be actors. They are coached on how to lean into the camera while on the air in an attempt to better engage viewers and to use their hands, fingers outstretched, to somehow suggest more meaning and passion to their words in much the same style of people selling used cars, cleaning supplies, and discount furniture on TV commercials. I saw one TV reporter who was so animated and dramatic that he reminded me of a spoof of a ubiquitous salesman of discount furniture and appliances on late-night TV. So much for journalism's time-honored tradition of dispassionate reporting.

Television news coaches today tell reporters and anchor people where and how to stand in order to convey more meaning in their on-air appearances. One trainer told me that he wants to see reporters stand in front of an open door or window, when possible, to suggest depth in what they are saying on the air. I listened patiently, resisting the urge to suggest that he was out of his mind.

Today's TV reporters are also coached and rehearsed on ways to use their voice to communicate real care and sincerity for what they are saying even though their words might not. It's not unlike what a film or stage actor does to rehearse for a theatrical part, except TV news people are reporting news of the day. They are intentionally putting editorial spin and bias on news stories with voice inflection.

It's a method of sounding sympathetic or exuberant to create some level of drama by emphasizing the wrong words and ending thoughts or sentences with your voice going up in pitch, rather than the customary drop. I bet you would think twice about inviting someone into your living room who came to the front door and spoke in such a contrived, pretentious manner. If you do invite them in, better hide the silver.

Normal people don't communicate that way with one another, and it sounds odd on the air even though it's become an accepted style. To me, this new style of speaking in television news, copied by many reporters and newsreaders, reminds me of those nursery-rhyme recordings my children listened to years ago that featured the voice of a woman who seemed to be talking down to my children in a simple and patronizing manner.

I am often asked during strategic communications workshops why it is that local TV news reporters can't get their facts correct when they report stories given to them by public relations professionals. It's not surprising; inaccuracy has become a signature of local TV newscasts. Pitching stories to local TV news reporters is always a roll of the dice … and more often than not, you'll lose.

The reality is that many local TV reporters, always with an eye on maybe making it big-time on a network or cable channel, are more consumed with concocting stories that convey shock, fear, and gore—the standard formula of local television news today—and with career enhancement than with delivering well-balanced stories.

News departments quietly pay consultants for story angles designed to hype newscast audience numbers, especially during rating periods—the infamous sweeps, when audience-viewing habits are sampled to measure the competitive forces within each television market. Capturing the coveted number one spot allows a station to charge the highest amount for commercials.

Here's a real example. A local television news team in Washington, D.C., singled out a real estate company at random for a concocted "investigative" story about possible fair-housing violations during a ratings sweeps period. There was nothing investigative about the story. In fact there wasn't even a story, because there had been no complaints and the company had done nothing wrong.

The reporter got the idea, not from a local tip about something possibly being awry, but from an out-of-town TV news consultant who suggested the story to hype ratings. The story angle had been decided before the reporter and cameraperson even left the TV station.

What appeared on the air was out of context, full of innuendo, and inaccurate. The story was merely intended to boost ratings. It suggested there was a fair-housing problem in the community when none existed. Yet it managed to alarm local officials and civic leaders, and it smeared the real estate company's image. This sort of reporting by local television happens every day in cities across America. It is ethically dishonest, in my opinion, because it tricks audience perceptions.

My advice is always to first take your stories to either a newspaper or wire service first, where a higher level of journalistic integrity still exists. In fact, one of the best ways to get your story on local television news in the most accurate manner possible is to first get the story in print. Television news decision makers—network, local, and cable— have traditionally felt more comfortable running a story that first appeared in print.

A producer for ABC News told me that the fierce competitiveness of her industry breeds insecurity in the TV news business. Newscast producers want to feel safe when they make decisions on which story will make it on the air, she said. So they are more comfortable running stories that first appeared in the newspaper. She said a print story seems to "validate" the importance of the story for TV.

For as long as anyone can remember, it has often been the habit of television news to follow or react to major stories that first appeared in newspapers. A big story appears on the front page of the morning paper, and throughout the day and into the evening, it's recycled by television news, often with little new information.

This means that the news industry, operating in a fiercely competitive arena, has lost both the interest and pulse of its audiences and is searching frantically for ways to attract them back. Audiences have too many choices these days to find out what's happening in the world ... or to be entertained.

Former CNN Anchorman Aaron Brown said, "Television is the most perfect democracy. You sit there with your remote control and vote." This is good for audiences yet bad for news organizations; it is clearly a challenge when trying to achieve the strategic communications results we—and our stakeholders—expect.

"We're in a period of change and dislocation," said Tom Rosenstiel of Columbia University's Graduate School of Journalism. "Clearly, some of the older media are suffering."

Trust in news sources is down drastically, according to a study by the Project for Excellence in Journalism.

The State of the News Media 2008, funded by Pew Charitable Trusts, reveals dramatic seismic changes underway within the media:

- News is shifting from being a product to becoming a service delivered by today's newspaper, Web site, or newscast—how can you help me, even empower me? There is no single or *finished* news product anymore. As news consumption becomes continual, more new effort is put into producing incremental updates, as brief as 40-character e-mails sent from reporters directly to consumers without editing.

- A news organization and a news Web site are no longer final destinations. Now they must move toward also being stops along the way, gateways to other places, and a means to drill deeper, all ideas that connect to service rather than product. "The walled garden is over," the editor of one of the most popular news sites in the country said. A site restricted to its own content takes on the character of a cul de sac street with yellow "No Outlet" sign, reducing its value to the user. Providing the ability to search for more information has become the predominant paradigm.

- The prospects for user-created content, once thought possibly central to the next era of journalism, for now appear more limited, even among "citizen" sites and blogs. News people report the most promising parts of citizen input currently are new ideas, sources, comments and to some extent pictures and video. But citizens posting news content has proven less valuable, with too little that is new or verifiable.

- The agenda of the American news media continues to narrow, not broaden. A firm grip on this is difficult but the trends seem inescapable. A comprehensive audit of coverage shows that in 2007, two overriding stories—the war in Iraq and the 2008 presidential campaign—filled more than a quarter of the news hole (the amount of content a news provider needs to create in every news or publishing cycle) and seemed to consume much of the media's energy and resources. And what wasn't covered was in many ways as notable as what was. Other than Iraq—and to a lesser degree Pakistan and Iran—there was minimal coverage of events overseas, some of which directly involved U.S. interests, blood, and treasure. At the same time, consider the list of the domestic issues that each filled less than a single percent of the news hole: education, race, religion, transportation, the legal system, housing, drug trafficking, gun control, welfare, Social Security, aging, labor, abortion and more.

- Madison Avenue, rather than pushing change, appears to be having trouble keeping up with it. Like legacy media, advertising agencies have their own history, mores, and cultures that keep them from adapting to new technology and new consumer behavior. The people who run these agencies know the old-media methods and have old-media contacts. New media offer the promise of more detailed knowledge of consumer behavior, but the metrics are still evolving and empirical data have not yet delivered a clear path. Advertising executives, in other words, do not have answers any more than the news professionals.

In the newspaper business, the decades-long battle at the top between idealists and accountants is now over. Money talks; the idealists have lost. There is, however, a problem—the traditional advertising revenue is no longer there for mainstream media. Advertising dollars are swarming to New Media sites online. Not surprisingly, there is a sense of desperation in the newspaper business over what to do and how to survive. So, what is the future of the media in America?

The State of the American News Media in 2007—also funded by the Pew organization—revealed, "In a sense all news organizations are becoming more niche players, basing their appeal less on how they cover the news and more on what they cover."

- Blogging is on the brink of a new phase that will probably include scandal, profitability for some, and a splintering into elites and non-elites over standards and ethics. The use of blogs by political campaigns has intensified during presidential elections. Corporate public relations efforts are beginning to use blogs as well, often covertly. What gives blogging its authenticity and momentum—its open access—also makes it vulnerable to being used and manipulated.

- While journalists are becoming more serious about the Web, no clear models of how to do journalism online really exist yet, and some qualities are still only marginally explored.

- The key question is whether the investment community sees the news business as a declining industry or an emerging one in transition. If one believes that news will continue to be the primary public square where people gather—with the central newsrooms in a community delivering that audience across different platforms—then it seems reasonable that the economics in time will sort themselves out.

The new paradox of journalism today is more outlets covering fewer stories and the overarching challenge of finding ways to connect to today's changing audiences while making money. As the number of online places delivering news proliferates, the audience for each tends to shrink and the number of journalists in each organization, including mainstream media, is reduced.

Overall we have seen significant, almost shocking, waves of layoffs at daily newspapers in recent years. We're not buying newspapers the way we once did and cherished advertising budgets are not what they once were, a trend that is diluted even more today by cable, the Internet, and other forms of communication with large audiences.

Many mainstream media companies are deeply in debt. Nearly every week, we hear of more layoffs at newsrooms across the country. During one week in late June 2008, as a vivid example, almost 1,000 jobs were eliminated in the American newspaper industry, perhaps the bloodiest week yet for media job cuts in a year that saw many papers fighting for their lives.

"You read about the great names—the *Baltimore Sun*, the *Boston Globe*, the *Los Angeles Times*, the *San Jose Mercury News*—as if reading the obituary page," wrote columnist Timothy Egan for the *New York Times*.

When investor Sam Zell bought the Tribune Company, including the *Los Angeles Tribune* and the *Chicago Tribune*, he announced deep cuts, including in the newsrooms. The dozen newspapers owned by the Tribune were told to trim a total of 500 pages of news each week.

"With department stores consolidating both their operations and their advertising and with readers canceling the newspapers that land on their doorstep in favor of more instant gratification of the Web," David Carr wrote in the *New York Times*, "big newspapers full of deep reporting and serious ambitions seem like dinosaurs at the beginning of a very cold age."

A similar trend is clear in television. The number of correspondents employed by the evening newscasts is down more than 33 percent from 1985, and the number of overseas bureaus has been cut to less than half … or even worse.

The result, according to a Columbia University study of today's media, is "jumbled, chaotic, partial quality in some reports, without much synthesis…of the information." As the satirist Jon Stewart has observed, much of television news has turned into a "nonsensical gong show."

Respected television journalists who are put in the position of working in today's entertainment news environment often jump back in shock.

The highly acclaimed public affairs channel C-SPAN and the cable news giant CNN once teamed up temporarily in a cooperative venture that seemed to have benefits for both parties—greater public awareness for C-SPAN and greater respectability for CNN. It meant that C-SPAN hosts would work stints as news anchors on CNN. The arrangement didn't last long.

C-SPAN chief operating officer and program host Susan Swain told me that when she briefly took up on-air duties at CNN, there was little time to focus on the stories as a responsible journalist. The frantic production pace, the distractions of reading to the precise timing of promotional music and CNN's various computer-generated sound effects—intended to build anticipation for upcoming stories— overshadowed clarity in reporting news. It was all about generating excitement and drama, she observed. It was show business.

It's no different at the other cable and satellite news channels. The once respected lines between news, shameless promotion, contrived and staged reality shows, and commercials are today no more than a blur, making it difficult for a viewer to discern between hype for the news story, hype for an advertiser, or hype for entertainment programming. Communicating the news of the day in a clear and accurate manner takes a backseat.

With the exception of the *NewsHour* with Jim Lehrer on PBS and original news programming on HDNet Television, and original news programming on HDNet Television, many news stories on television networks, local stations, and cable channels are intentionally designed to be more dramatic through the use of sound effects and music that might fit the mood of stories, according to news producers. Among all the swoosh and swish noises that augment the drama of today's TV newscasts, a reporter friend called my attention to one sound effect on the cable news channel MSNBC that seemed very similar to that of a toilet flushing. He was right. Whether that sound speaks for the state of television news today is another matter.

Newscast producers today make an auditory editorial impact using the same sound effects used in the production of action-packed major motion pictures. It all began with a video editing device called Avid that allowed producers of motion pictures to enhance the visual impact of a scene with unusual, dramatic, and seemingly unreal sound effects. If you've been to an action movie in recent years, you no doubt have experienced the floor-shaking sonic booms and heightened sound effects. Chances are that came from an Avid or a similar special-effects device.

From major motion pictures, the sound effects moved to television sports to boost the impact, and then into regular television programs and eventually to newscasts, adding to today's blur between entertainment and news on television. What's real, and what's not? Only the sound-effects editor knows. Here's the dilemma: Special effects in a motion picture can be cool and exciting. Using sound effects to bring drama to television news is editorializing and manipulating the effect of the news.

Ethical conduct on television news programs has come a long way from the meticulous set of policies developed by Richard Salant, the popular president of the CBS News division in the 1970s who wanted the credibility of news separated from sports and other entertainment projects. His directives prohibited the editorial use of music and sound effects on any news program. Sadly those days are gone.

Today's news business is increasingly opinionated and salacious, with the driving forces of news leaders locked in competitive struggles. The only constant about the news media today is change, as one reporter remarked.

It is in this environment that today's media savvy professional is seeking to build awareness. If you are getting the impression that we've got to be fast on our feet to get our story before a moving target, you're darn right. It's more challenging and more competitive than ever before to get the media's attention and achieve accurate, responsible, and meaningful coverage. The task requires a savvy understanding of news media trends and relationship-building methods to get to know journalists.

While it used to be that all we needed to do was give a reporter a good idea for a story and they'd run with it, today we must be prepared to provide a lot more, including anything that will help a reporter convince his or her editor that the story is worthwhile and relevant.

The discipline of professional strategic communications today requires that we nurture the story-development process even after we've found interest from a journalist.

We must be prepared to provide all kinds of background information, details, and guidance to a reporter, while always keeping the focus on how we would like the story to come out. More often than not, we need to do the legwork for a newsperson in order for it to happen—something unheard of just a few years ago. It's often time-consuming, but necessary, and the payoff is big when you land great coverage.

Here's a tip: If you want to control the news angle of a story you are taking to the media, write it first. Draft a story of about 300 to 400 words in length and really work to make it read like a legitimate story, exactly like something you might want to read in tomorrow's newspaper. Then, when you pitch the story to a reporter, you will have a better focus of how the story elements—the interviews, facts, background information, and other viewpoints—should come together for the reporter you have approached. Heck, you might even give the draft to the reporter under the guise of "background materials." I bet you will find that parts of your own version just may appear in the reporter's final story.

Is strategic communications worth all the effort? You bet! The news media, despite its sometimes rocky and profit-driven evolution over the last couple of decades, remains the most powerful form of communication in America—second only to a couple of people swapping gossip over the office water cooler. So let's get in the ring and work to make news.

Effective strategic communications in today's world mandates that communicators—including public relations people who deal with the media—work harder than ever to understand how stories occur and how news happens. Communications people also need to try, whenever possible, to stay ahead of trends in news coverage.

Public relations people need "a reality check," said Linda Ellerbee, a television reporter, anchor, and producer with more than three decades of distinguished work. "We are in the middle of a seismic shift in how we, and the rest of the world, receive our news," she said.

Today's news in general, and television news in particular, is more focused on immediacy than accuracy, Ellerbee said.

Neal Shapiro, executive producer of "Dateline NBC" for many years, agrees. He shared with me during a dinner in New York that television news is solely about "ratings, ratings, ratings." That's how his program decides what stories to air. Whatever story will attract the biggest audience is the story that television news will report.

Of course what he's saying is that "ratings, ratings, ratings" translates into "money, money, money" for NBC.

When the heiress Paris Hilton was released from jail after being convicted of drunk driving, Larry King's show producers and CNN executives threw around enormous clout and called in favors to have her on their program first. Why, other than ratings, would they do that?

Gone are the days when the purpose of news was purely to inform. Instead, the quest for sensation, ratings, and the resulting money directly drives editorial content.

Cable news often flashes up large, red "Breaking News" banners to tell us that troubled celebrities have another court appearance or have entered a detoxification center. Fox News interrupted national programming for nearly 20 minutes to show police chasing a man who had stolen a car in southern California.

You can see that today's media environment is curious and at times laughable, making it fodder for comedians like Jon Stewart, host of the *Daily Show* on the Comedy Central channel.

In our work to become media savvy and to capture attention for what we have to say, telling our story, and making news, we face stiff competition. There are new challenges at every turn. Someone or some event of the day is always out there with a sexier angle or more timely approach.

At my strategic communications firm, I coached our younger team members about techniques for approaching the media by saying the team members either needed to take the time to establish trusted contacts in the media or learn to accept rejection gracefully.

For either an executive or a communications professional, an essential element of building influence and credibility in today's media world is to establish a network of contacts and make the effort to communicate with them on a regular basis.

We must remain open to new trends, approaches and ideas in the media. We need to be aware of the media's never-ending appetite for some new and different twist on a story, the current flavor of the day. And we should never take it personally when we are get turned down.

Getting your story before the media can be done, but smart planning and hard work are required to really understand how the news media operates today and what it desires. While seismic changes are causing the tradition mainstream media to shake at its foundations and scramble to rebuild, exciting new media outlets are coming online. Politico.com, for example, has quickly become a credible and influential political news source, not only in Washington but nationwide. Another online site, the Center for Independent Media (NewJournalist.org) is helping to redefine the media of tomorrow by focusing on critical underreported stories in cities and communities across America.

While the media retrenches, new opportunities are created for the leaders of savvy organizations to get their messages heard and to create leadership. But, as I have mentioned previously, today's best communicators are storytellers, and, as you will see in the next chapter, they know how to cultivate influential contacts.

CHAPTER TEN

IT'S ALL ABOUT WHO YOU KNOW

Journalists don't give most people in public relations high marks for knowing how to develop a legitimate news story, getting the story before the news media, and cultivating trusted relationships with reporters and editors.

Reporters want trusted sources for stories and most I have interviewed are open to relationships with public relations people who can be a source of news for their beat or coverage area. But, reporters would prefer that their trusted sources be the leader of an organization … the boss. Developing these working relationships with the media is critical to getting the results you expect, and, as I have mentioned previously, it is not always a good idea to delegate.

Judy Feldman of *Money* magazine was succinct when she told me, "It's always great to be able to call someone who you know and ask, 'What's up?'"

Many public relations agencies, however, are media-challenged when it comes to effectively getting the word out about clients. As I previously mentioned, internal training programs at even the largest PR agencies are woefully lacking or do not exist. Their media relations efforts have remained stalled for too long, bogged down by predictability and traditional tactics, and simply not keeping pace with today's fast-changing media world. These efforts often come up short in the areas of authentic, trusted media relationships, journalistic skills, and the knowledge of what makes news.

All too often the key assignment of pitching stories to the media is handed to the youngest members of a public relations agency who may have little or no training or preparation.

So many PR firms suffer from a counterproductive dichotomy: Their clients expect the professionals to have the media contacts and skills. Yet too many agency executives consider pitching reporters to be beneath them, and the execs hand off the assignment to junior employees and interns with little or no training to actually do the work, sink or swim.

"Sometimes they sound as bored and rote as a telemarketer, and you know the PR agency has dispensed an intern to read off a sheet," said Linda Stasi, a columnist at the *New York Post*. "Don't waste my precious daily deadline time like this. It's not fair to me, and it's not fair to the poor intern who probably gets the brunt of it all!"

On one hand, media relations at most agencies is bread and butter, yet on the other hand the work is treated as, well, a bother, as if the agency employees had better things to do. The message is clear that many agencies have gotten lazy about the changing styles of strategic communications. Therein is a big opportunity for anyone who wants to do a better job.

In response to client concerns, improving strategic communications skills has been targeted as a top priority by several major public relations agencies in the United States and Britain. Clients have an ever-increasing need to reach audiences through the media in a timely way. Unquestionably, corporate clients of PR firms, constantly seeking a competitive edge, want strategic counsel and lofty ideas. But they also want the immediate payoff of effective strategic communications.

Clients expect public relations experts to have deep media connections and close working relationships with the most powerful journalists, whether in times of crisis or for routine product promotion. That is just not the case at so many PR agencies. In fact, many agencies—particularly the larger ones—provide little training for the junior-level people most often assigned the task of pitching the media because each hour of training takes away a billable hour of work.

"Media relations," said Brian Lamb, founder and chief executive officer of C-SPAN, "is about relationships. A reporter needs to know who you are. It's as important as what you have to say. If you have a great announcement but have not established a contact or relationship in the media, no one will pay attention."

Lamb's powerful words get incisively to the core of effective strategic communications today. It's all about establishing relationships with journalists. But it's hard for PR people to develop those relationships if they don't understand how people in the media operate.

Public relations people "are not sensitive enough to deadlines," National Public Radio's Barbara Bradley Hagerty told me. "They don't bother to ask, to find out whether you are in the middle of something; they just launch into a pitch. Most public relations people don't know how journalists work. Most PR people are not quick enough in responding."

Michele Chandler, a technology reporter for the *Mercury News* in San Jose, told me that she would primarily encourage PR representatives to make sure they are sending pitches to the proper people. "I routinely receive e-mails and phone pitches for healthcare-related stories, a beat I have not had in years," she said.

Her message is clear: Meaningful results from your efforts in media relations happen when you get to know the right people in the media.

Chandler recommends that people "query first by e-mail, unless you absolutely, positively know the reporter and what beat they cover. When doing a follow-up call, be prepared to back up why the particular event or person or company you're pitching is newsworthy or whether what's being highlighted is part of a wider trend."

In other words, she, like all other journalists, is looking for timely news with a purpose. If your story signals the leading edge of a trend, all the better.

Jim Brady, the executive editor of WashingtonPost.com, has a clever suggestion for executives and communications people, alike, to take advantage of a popular trend and stay in contact with journalists who cover their organizations: use Facebook, an informal and mutual online meeting place. Chances are that many of the reporters you know already have Facebook accounts. Invite reporters and bloggers to join your Facebook group, Brady advises, and exchange personal messages and information there about your organization.

But, therein is another challenge for the public relations agency business. Many PR agencies have only lately recognized the enormous communications opportunities presented online, and consequently, are late on the learning curve.

The head of a global PR firm told me not long ago during a conference that she hates e-mail and doesn't understand the Internet. Unfortunately, her lack of online savvy has impeded her entire agency's growth into the world of New Media. To paraphrase a popular phrase, that PR agency is practicing analog communications in a digital world.

Journalists show their frustration when they share their difficulties in dealing with PR people. If a story goes wrong, what most often happens is the impulse to heap blame on the reporter, when the reality of the situation is that the story might not have been accurately pitched or communicated to the news media in the first place. Journalists also feel bombarded with pitches that are completely irrelevant to what they do.

NPR's Jean Cochran has a pet peeve with all the people trying to pitch her with stories that they think would be "perfect" for NPR. She gets literally hundreds of e-mails each week from people who want stories about their cause or product on the popular news and information radio network.

"I'm not the person to approach," she told me. "Please explain to readers of your book, David, that I only focus on the latest news of the day for my newscasts. It's a tight schedule to do seven newscasts each day. People with hopes of getting their feature stories on the air somehow get the idea that because they hear me read the newscasts, I might be interested in their stories for all of NPR. They need to learn that I am the wrong person to pitch with their feature ideas. I don't have time to track down their feature stories, and their e-mails only clog my inbox."

The problem is usually simple: Public relations people just have not invested the time to know how the news media works, what the journalists need for a story idea, who to contact in the media, or how to make a story pitch.

What I have found while speaking with executives in preparation for this book is that the leaders who are most visible, recognized, and respected in their industries have taken the time to establish their own network of media connections. Each day, they exchange e-mails and phone calls with reporters, often completely unrelated from the efforts of their internal corporate communications departments. These leaders have their own trusted relationships with journalists who cover their industry and freely exchange ideas, knowledge, news, and, yes, sometimes gossip. This approach is very smart and leads to shared respect and mutual benefits. Journalists gain exclusive access to industry leaders and executives establish opportunities to enhance the image of their leadership and the reputations of their organizations.

I love to tell this story while speaking before groups about today's changing media and the new brand management approaches we need to find: A group of University of Delaware Cooperative Extension educators and scientists, who are not PR people, decided to take matters into their own hands to find new ways to improve relations with the news media in their state.

Their goal was to see more of their stories in the local media and the way they handled the project was impressive by any measure. Their first step was to ask a group of journalists to meet with them, face-to-face, and give them the straight story about how the media works. I was lucky enough to attend as a guest.

The session took place at Rehoboth, Delaware, a location that was remote enough to be a couple of hours' drive for most people, including the reporters. I had the honor to be invited to attend by Dr. Jan Seitz, a highly respected leader of the 4-H youth development organization in Delaware and nationwide, who is also a friend.

The session revealed the professional commitments of all involved to enhance the reputation of their news organizations and trade.

Watching the interchange, I was struck by the realization of how seldom public relations agencies and corporation communications departments meet in such a forum to learn new trends and techniques and to build relationships. Yet a group of University of Delaware educators and scientists had figured out how to get better coverage.

The journalists represented the spectrum of the news media in Delaware and included Luladey Tadesse, a business reporter for the *News Journal* in Wilmington, Delaware; Jenni Pastusak, a reporter and anchor at WBOC television news in Salisbury, Maryland; and Dennis Forney, publisher of the *Cape Gazette* in Lewes, Delaware.

Pastusak explained the need for local television news to come up with stories that appeal primarily to women, age 25 to 35. That's her audience, and the target of the station's advertising. At her TV station, stories are aimed at an imaginary viewer named "Lisa" who wants to know about threats to her family, such as a new flu outbreak, who will stop what she is doing to watch stories about health issues and well-being and who will be touched by news features with "hard-hitting" emotional appeal. Pastusak underscored the importance of news sources, saying that she calls people she knows in the community to get stories for her newscasts.

The signal was clear that local television news in "the world of Lisa," as Pastusak described it, might not appeal to all of us, but it's where local television is today. It might not be the depth of reporting we would like to see, but in America, it is formula-driven local TV that brings in advertising dollars.

Tadesse, who originally worked at the *Los Angeles Times* before coming to Delaware, spoke of building her network of news contacts throughout the state with ordinary people she had met while doing business stories—people who became trusted resources for other stories. Again, it's all about relationships.

Dennis Forney was the old-timer in the group. He's been a respected newspaperman in Delaware for over three decades. His definition of news is simple: Give him a timely story he hasn't heard before and put a human face on it. Don't send him a news release, just pick up the phone and give him a call. News releases don't result in news stories. And personal contact with the news media helps you cut through competitive clutter and be noticed.

The common message that these journalists shared with the University of Delaware group was that reporters today rely on solid, trusted contacts and sources—relationships, in other words—to develop stories. Relationships. It's all about who you know in the media and what they need for a story and making whatever you present timely and relevant.

Then there are those journalists you cannot approach with a story pitch. This group includes many editorial writers, columnists, and broadcast anchor people. It's hit or miss, of course, but usually comes down to your personal relationship as a credible news source to the newsperson.

Frank Rich at the *New York Times* shared with me, "My column is self-generated, and when I deal with PR people, it's at my instigation, not theirs—usually because I want specific information." As he said that, I thought … *and the PR people Frank Rich is likely to call are people he knows and trusts.* Yes, it's all about relationships and who you know.

During my research for this book, a well-known editorial writer at the *New York Times* politely declined my request to discuss media relations, because he does not want to reveal his news-gathering and writing style. I completely respect his position. Nonetheless, he is one of the most open and accessible editorial writers on the planet, and in a quiet, subtle manner, he disclosed something about his style: He is reachable; he is open. You can contact him. It's not done through an expensive, customized news-release service but rather on the direct personal level of simply sending him an e-mail. He responded to me within an hour.

Strategic communications nonetheless remains a mystery for many executives and PR practitioners. It is a seemingly vague thing that often involves hiring an agency to do something intangible, that may or may not have any results. It is common to hear company executives express their displeasure to their public relations people and agency at having spent vast sums of money on media relations campaigns that totally miss the mark.

Many journalists are fully aware that corporations often fumble and miss excellent opportunities to be heard and gain valuable publicity when their public relations people don't have the right connections and knowledge of the media.

Andrew Buncombe, Washington correspondent for London's *The Independent* newspaper, said, "Sometimes I cannot believe the opportunities that big companies let pass when I am seeking a comment from them on a story that is at worst neutral and at best very much in their favor. Some (public relations people) are pathetic."

The most important thing, Buncombe said, "is to understand the market and understand the media outlet you are trying to pitch the story to. No media organization operates without a degree of bias in the stories they promote. The PR person needs to study that."

There are many stories, however, of how media-aware public relations professionals have helped big companies capture the moment.

Here's one: During the mega-merger of the railroad giants, Conrail and CSX Transportation, the team at Edelman Worldwide that was working on behalf of CSX became keenly aware that safety was the top issue. The Federal Railroad Administration (FRA) had said that its primary concern in blessing the merger was whether the deal would result in a safe railroad operation that would serve most of the eastern half of the United States. The Edelman folks knew that reporters, who would talk with FRA officials, would pick up on the government's emphasis on safety.

Consequently, the issue of whether the CSX-Conrail merger would result in a safe railroad dominated Edelman's omnibus strategic plan to help CSX through the lengthy merger process. Working with the railroad, the public relations firm staged on-site safety demonstrations for the news media. Edelman was proactive in addressing safety concerns that cities and communities had over the possibility of a greater number of trains that might be running through their towns. Reporters who visited CSX offices were shown how the company planned to merge not only two railroads but also two railroad cultures into a safe new operation.

Interview talking points for CSX spokespersons, backed up by pinpoint data, emphasized how the railroad merger would create the opportunity for American industry to be more cost efficient by shipping large amounts of goods by rail. Savings could even be passed along to consumers. And shipping by rail would reduce the number of trucks on highways. Fewer heavy trucks competing for roadway space with motorists would make it safer for all drivers. Safety was also underscored in briefings for Wall Street analysts in New York and before lawmakers on Capitol Hill in Washington.

In the end, when the FRA approved the merger, the federal agency praised CSX for its emphasis on creating an environment where safety was the number one priority. The government regulators commended CSX for effectively communicating the importance of safety throughout the cultures of both companies and across the entire rail system.

Naturally, because the safety issue was the top priority of the federal watchdog agency and underscored in all their statements to the media, the work done by CSX made positive headlines and dominated the extensive media coverage.

"Successful PR people have a 'service' attitude, as opposed to one based on 'spin control,'" commented longtime Washington, D.C., newspaperman Lyle Denniston. "And successful people understand that 'service' means melding their assistance to the media with loyally serving their client. The two can go together."

Clearly, in the example of Edelman Worldwide's work with CSX Transportation, service—assistance and a close working relationship with the media—was an essential factor for achieving success.

Overall, when I talked with journalists about the value of strategic communications to their work in the news business, I found a healthy attitude. Journalists do need people who will give them good stories on a regular basis. They are open to ideas and to covering legitimate and relevant news events. And they believe that public relations people can make a significant contribution to both helping their clients or employers build favorable awareness and to providing valuable assistance to the media.

As Scott Simon, the popular host of "Weekend Edition" on National Public Radio, told me, "You are part of an honorable profession. The sanctimony of so many of us journalists aside, I think there is probably about the same proportion of scoundrels to saints in both lines. Cheerfulness counts for a lot."

The first tenet of effective strategic communications is to passionately embrace the reality that it's a relationship-driven discipline. It really is about who you know in the media and the level of trust and respect you have developed. A healthy measure of good humor never hurts.

CHAPTER ELEVEN

ONLY THING CONSTANT IS CHANGE

There were several sea-change events—starting in late 2004—that have made a profound impact on journalism and the way news is covered. The events raised important questions, including who is a journalist in today's changing world, and how can we in the business of strategic communications better communicate with them?

The answers involve learning new techniques. But we need to move quickly, and we have a lot to learn. It begins by letting go of the bygone notion that anyone in the news media is influenced by traditional approaches that have been attempted by PR people, such as shoveling press materials at the media.

The first event was a tsunami that roared over islands and populated coastal areas in Asia and east Africa, killing tens of thousands of people without warning. The images of the sea devouring whole communities that aired on television news around the world were taken mostly by tourists, not news crews, who were lucky enough to be in higher locations and who had the presence of mind to pick up their digital cameras and shoot.

The second event was the series of terrorist bombings in London, England, on July 7, 2005, and the third was Hurricane Katrina, which devastated New Orleans, Louisiana, and the Gulf Coast.

Each event had the effect of creating a new type of journalist: "citizen journalists," ordinary people like you and me who are witnesses to news in the making. These events shook up mainstream and New Media news organizations and forced them to recognize that the forces of news, technology, and reality have altered the face of journalism forever.

For anyone who seeks to attract and control the media's attention, the events presented new opportunities and new methods of communicating more influentially than ever through the media. Strategic communications methods are evolving seemingly at light speed. The message is clear: Stop mailing out all those news releases and watch the trends.

When the July 7 bombs detonated in the London tube, eyewitness video—the only video available of the explosions—was taken by passengers who switched their cell or mobile phones to video mode and took dramatic pictures. When editors at BBC Television news became aware of the grainy yet spellbinding video, the decision was immediately made to put those images on the air as quickly as possible. The riveting video was broadcast around the world, driving home the horror of terrorism for many of us.

"The London bombs of 7/7 changed the business of broadcast news forever," Jon Williams, a senior editor at BBC Television News, wrote me in an e-mail. "For the first time, the audience became 'citizen journalists' en-masse by sending their mobile phone pictures—stills and video—by SMS [cell phone text messaging] and e-mail.

"Potentially everyone is a journalist. If something goes wrong—if something happens—someone, somewhere will capture it on a mobile phone. Whether it's the queues outside Heathrow airport because of the British Airways strike, or a bus driver caught abusing a passenger, there's no hiding place for organizations any more."

Within hours of the July 7 bombings, the BBC was alerting viewers and listeners about special Internet links where witnesses could upload any pictures or video they had captured. Response was overwhelming, and the venerable British news institution quickly found their coverage ahead of competitors, all because their viewers had become their reporters.

It is my personal observation that this almost instant partnership between an audience and the BBC speaks volumes about citizens' devotion to and respect for the news operations of the British Broadcasting Corporation. It is a loyalty that today eludes television news organizations in the United States, partly because there are far more choices for getting news in America.

There's a larger reason for the audience disenfranchisement in the United States. So many broadcast news outfits in America—which focus on delivering news that is consultant- and formula-driven—have isolated themselves from what is relevant and meaningful in their respective communities and from their audiences.

As many media relations specialists know all too well, it's often a challenge to reach the right person at a TV or radio newsroom. For the average citizen, who may have a legitimate news story but lacks the unlisted telephone numbers, it's nearly impossible. So while the local "Eyewitness News" may promote themselves as "on your side" and "working harder for you," they have not, in all honesty, worked to reach out and earn the loyalty of their audiences. That isolationist behavior by broadcast newsrooms is beginning to turn around out of necessity for survival.

A couple of months after the terrorist bombings in London, an enormous hurricane named Katrina struck the Gulf Coast and the city of New Orleans. The devastation was beyond comprehension. As fierce winds blew and the storm surge leveled towns along the coast, amateur photographers, armed with their MiniDV video cameras and digital still cameras normally intended for home movies and pictures of the kids, captured effects of the historic storm.

A few television news organizations appealed to these citizen journalists to share their pictures, and even though the response was not as overwhelming as the London bombings, what the U.S. television news organizations received was some of the most graphic and dramatic video and digital still photos of the storm and its aftermath.

Jerry Kay of Environmental News Network points to the fact that a news assignment that once required a $20,000 video camera can now be reported using a cell phone.

"Amazingly, some of the first and most striking images of Hurricane Katrina were actually captured by cell phones," he said. "Anyone can be a producer and use video as a way of communicating a mission, conveying a message, or sharing a passion with the world."

What caught my attention during the Katrina disaster was a fresh openness of the news media to accepting visual coverage from ordinary folks, like you and me. Even if you were a public relations person who had outstanding and relevant video of a news event, the media would likely be open to airing your pictures with full knowledge that you might be working to promote a client.

This was the same television news media that was up in arms a few months earlier after it was revealed that Ketchum Public Relations had manufactured fake news under a hefty federal contract on behalf of the political agenda of the George W. Bush administration. Ketchum had produced video news releases or VNRs that were distributed to television newsrooms across the country to promote the No Child Left Behind or NCLB law on behalf of the Department of Education. The whole scheme to sell NCLB, which included journalist payola, was subsequently labeled "covert propaganda" by the Government Accountability Office. Just a year earlier, Ketchum had another government contract to produce phony video news releases to hype the Bush administration's new approach to Medicare, and that too blew up in a controversy over whether to use taxpayer money to create fake news reports in support of a government agenda.

Video news releases have been sent out by organizations for decades as a way to get specific messages and images on television newscasts, and if the story is good, it has a chance of getting on the air. But the No Child Left Behind and Medicare stunts had the effect of poisoning the well for the whole concept of legitimate video news releases. Overnight, television news operations got skittish and stopped airing them for a while until the flap cooled off. Television news has a short memory and once again airs worthwhile and appealing video, regardless of the source.

Incidentally, the No Child Left Behind scandal was not limited just to bogus video news releases. The Education Department, working through Ketchum Public Relations, paid nationally syndicated television show commentator Armstrong Williams $241,000 to help promote the Bush administration's education reform law on the air. *USA Today* reported that the campaign required Williams "to regularly comment on NCLB during the course of his broadcasts." Once again, the money was funneled through Ketchum Public Relations.

Such examples of subterfuge can rarely be concealed in today's digital revolution. We are in an era of transparency that demands truthfulness, openness, and integrity. In this case, the plot was exposed by the traditional mainstream news media and bloggers, alike.

Such stories of "payola," domestic propaganda, and bad judgment aside, newer opportunities to get your messages on television newscasts are opening, especially if you invest the time to develop a genuine, timely news story—the sort of story the media wants.

The openness of the media to reconsider and accept images from outside sources during the London bombings and Katrina signaled a change that merits notice by the public relations industry. While the days of a traditional video news release may well be nearly over, television news will air video from outside sources that is ... and this is very important ... timely, relevant and, most of all, compelling. The more exciting the video, the better.

A dynamic woman named Shoba Purushothaman is at the forefront of defining what part of the future of television news may look like, and what she sees will be transparent, truthful, and fast moving.

Purushothaman is founder and chief executive officer of TheNewsMarket.com, a New York-based company that describes itself as using the latest "Web technology to facilitate easy and efficient transfers of broadcast-standard digital video and other multimedia content from providers to journalists."

From my experience in television news, I would describe TheNewsMarket.com as a tactical digital platform that handles the logistics and technology of getting your video before a vast universe of traditional and New Media while you focus on strategy and messages. It is an online distributor of news video and editorial content from the business and nonprofit world.

The old-fashioned style of distributing video news releases to local TV newsrooms via expensive satellite feeds, as Ketchum did with its phony video stories, is on its way out. News video today is distributed far more economically and faster as online digital transfers in any technical format desired by broadcast TV, bloggers, and even newspapers.

With technical support facilities in her native India and in China, Purushothaman's TheNewsMarket.com is growing at a rate of 80 to 100 percent each year, distributing news video on behalf of clients that range from Airbus, Volvo, Nokia, and Adidas to the Red Cross, the World Bank, and UNICEF.

Purushothaman says her clients are organizations that recognize there are no boundaries anymore from a business perspective. She envisions a future news environment where traditional news hierarchies and middlemen will vaporize and organizations will have the ability to communicate their news directly to consumers, without intermediaries.

Whether it comes to that or not, we truly live in a flat global communications world today—exactly as Thomas L. Friedman wrote in his bestseller, *The World is Flat*—and the whole business of communicating news is being rethought, recalibrated, and reinvested. Breaking news in one market can instantly impact something around the world, and organizations need to be on alert and know how to use the latest tools of the New Media digital resolution to protect their brands and deliver accurate messages.

CHAPTER TWELVE

STRUGGLING TO FIND A PULSE

If you haven't guessed by now, there is a "seismic change," as journalists are calling it, in the news business that is on a roll and gaining momentum; it is driven mostly by technology that has made every instant a news cycle, younger audiences who are bombarded by more sources of information, and by leaders in the mass media who are concerned about economic storm clouds. In an industry where money often dictates the quality of the news reporting we see, executives are worried. Faced with competition for advertising dollars and competition from cable and the Internet, the traditional media is scrambling to assure a viable future.

"Hold on," you may say. "This sounds familiar ... countless other industries faced similar challenges and shakeouts around 2000." You would be correct, and those warning signs were out there then for the news business. It just took news executives a little longer to figure out that the earth was shifting out from underneath their feet. Some are still working on it.

CBS News is a prime example of a traditional mainstream news organization slow to change and searching for its audience.

Joe Gandelman of *The Moderate Voice* blog has written, "The biggest issue facing CBS is whether—and how—it can adjust a venerable news institution to the reality that we're living in the 21st century, and it may be time to explore changes in form as well as personnel."

The hiring of morning talk show host Katie Couric for tens of millions of dollars to anchor the network's "CBS Evening News" has failed to attract significant numbers of new viewers or rebuild the reputation of the once-great news organization. In fact, Couric's sometimes abrasive style has alienated and fracture whatever pride was left within CBS News.

CBS News clearly has lost the pulse and the interest of the iPhone-Facebook-Youtube generation. There are too many far more interesting channels of news-entertainment-escapism-whatever out there for most people to sit down at a scheduled time to bother watching Katie Couric or any of the other traditional evening television newscasts anchors, for that matter.

Ever-changing audience expectations, the merging of technologies, and the instantaneous 24-hour news cycle have only increased the amount of news and information available to consumers while decreasing the importance of traditional media—very likely spelling the demise of network and local news as we know it today.

For the news business, the jury is out—primarily because you and I are the jury—and we are faced with many new sources these days to get all the news and information we desire. To make matters worse, surveys show that we are also losing trust in the traditional news media.

Dan Gillmor, a former reporter for the *Mercury News* in San Jose and pioneer Web journalist, or blogger, said, "It's painful to watch a business I care so much about commit slow suicide this way. But the financial writing is increasingly on the wall for the industry that simply can't figure out how to handle its challenges." Yet Gillmor and other journalists see this change bringing tremendous new opportunities for more effective communications between public relations people and the news media.

Gillmor, who regularly offers sage advice to PR people, writes in his blog, *Bayosphere*, that for PR people, "traditional methods must give way to different kinds of conversations."

"But the key word here is 'conversation'—and the first rule is that you have to listen. That's why companies should encourage comments from those various constituencies, publicly and privately. A conversation doesn't mean total transparency, but it does mean a willingness to listen. We all have plenty to learn."

A study by the Annenberg Public Policy Center has shown that the American public is split about evenly on whether news organizations usually get their facts straight. The center quotes Geneva Overholser, a journalism professor and former *Washington Post* ombudsman, as saying, "this study reveals a worrisome divide between the public's view of journalism and journalists' own views of their work." In other words, reporters may think their work is sound and important, but we may not agree.

The Media Center at the American Press Institute started watching these trends long before the July 7 bombings and Katrina. They have pulled together a group of visionary journalists to watch the evolution of the news business, and the goal is to try to make sense of the trends. The media center's project is called We Media. The "we" is all of us: you, me and everyone else.

Their research is fascinating and begins at a very high perspective. They have found that only three communications exist. The first two of the three communication media predate technology and have mutually exclusive characteristics.

"*Interpersonal* communications," according to the media center, "is the first communication medium. We commonly know it as one person talking to one other person." That manner of communicating has been around for a long time. Its hallmark is that what's shared reflects a unique mix of interests and "each partisan equally shares control of the content."

"The second communication medium is what the mass of people colloquially refer to as 'media.' It is the *mass medium*." Newspapers and broadcasters fall into this category, because one person has sole control of the content. Other vehicles of the mass medium are theater, books, royal decrees, and speeches.

Here's the exciting part, especially when learning how to be more effective at strategic communications: There is a new communication medium that doesn't have the mutually exclusive advantages and disadvantages of the two previous forms.

The *new medium* of communication, according to the media center, "can simultaneously send an individually tailored message, edition, or program to everyone on a mass scale. And, it lets every participant equally share control," leveling the playing field between publisher and consumer. Either can be both. That's where a slice of journalism may be headed.

Web sites are not vehicles of this new medium because, for the most part, they merely push mostly passive information at an audience. The Web sites of many corporations and organizations as well as newspapers, magazines, and broadcasters are nothing more than "shovelware" from the mass medium. That means information and stories are shoveled or pushed in one direction—our direction—hoping we'll be interested. In fact, most Web sites are either passive, archival, shovelware, or a combination of all three. It's not a particularly appealing brew for today's more discriminating online public.

Blogs—online journals—are something else entirely. Blogs have grown from an outlet for tech-savvy geeks to an increasingly influential level of communications. Blogs are interactive. You can give feedback and you can comment. In fact, we are seeing that the more popular blogs are the more interactive ones that give readers a voice. That's participatory journalism and the concept has caught the news media's attention, big-time.

We are seeing news-oriented bloggers keeping mainstream journalists on their toes by carefully digging into the background of controversial stories and providing another level of fact-checking. Bloggers have done the job the more traditional reporters failed to tackle on stories, such as the use of white phosphorus as a chemical weapon by U.S. troops in Iraq or the provenance of the letters claiming to be from George W. Bush's commander in the National Guard—the flawed story that brought down the credibility of CBS News anchorman Dan Rather.

Blogs are new medium and have become a popular, powerful way of influencing reporters, columnists, and editors. Each day, respected journalists, from Frank Rich at the *New York Times* to Brit Hume at Fox News, quote something they've read in a blog.

There's the big opportunity for an organization that strives to be a leader in strategic communications: This seismic change trend in the news business opens the door for delivering our stories to the media and making news, so long as our stories are more legitimate, more timely, more relevant, and more compelling. Top executives and public relations people have the chance to join in as citizen journalists and provide the media with material, provided it's a real news story that we pitch to a specific reporter or news organization. No one is paying attention to self-serving, boring, and fluffy news announcements. The competition for audiences is too fierce. These are exciting new ways of making news.

While we hear journalists say they are open to these stories from outside sources, their message is also that we need to embrace new styles and technology for communicating with the media.

- Get away from traditional news releases if for no other reason than because reporters are buried in too many of them and ignore most of them.

- Only hold news conferences when we really, really have something important to say, and even then, find credible ways of covering our own news conferences for reporters who can't make it because of increased work demands.

- Watch the signs and remain open to emerging new trends in technology, like blogs and social networks, as a delivery method of updating the media with razor-edge timeliness.

- As an executive, personal contacts and relationships with journalists who cover your organization or industry are your most effective tool to manage the media.

The invitation from the media has been extended to those of us who make our living placing stories about our clients and employers in the news media. The media is perhaps more open than ever to partnering with us as long as we play by their rules and understand what they require. They make their livings reporting timely, legitimate news stories. Give them what they need to make news.

CHAPTER THIRTEEN

UNTANGLING ONLINE STRATEGIES AND WEB 2.0

Why should a leader or executive care about the online digital communications strategy of his or her organization? Why bother? What's the importance and the return on investment?

The answer is easy—everything. The future of most organizations today depends on effective online communications—the transparency of their messages matched with the methods of online communications—and how well they listen to and engage their audiences.

It is no longer pushing information at audiences or even being interactive. Today, we must seek to have personal conversations with audiences if we are to identify opportunities and respond to new trends.

Online communications technology has become a powerful force of change and collaboration within organizations. It enhances brand awareness and reputation management. It defines authentic leadership.

Visitors to Web sites today often make snap judgments about whether they are attracted to an organization or not based solely on an impression—their perception—of how the organization presents itself online. Visitors may ask themselves, "Is this someone I wish to do business with?" If an organization's Web site sends murky, ambiguous, or rambling messages, the downside can be serious.

Today, any company or organization has the ability to help chart the future through the clarity and transparency of its messages and how it utilizes the expanding spectrum of Web 2.0 online communications tools.

Web 2.0 is a new generation and evolving trend in World Wide Web technology and online design that helps organizations to not only interface more effectively with their audiences but takes communications to the level of personal conversation. The tools of Web 2.0 include blogs and dynamic content management sites that are an off-shoot of blog technology, wikis or online collaborative sharing of knowledge, podcasts, video, and social-networking sites such as MySpace, Facebook, and SecondLife.

Outpost Worldwide—a fast-growing high definition (HD) video production and independent motion picture company based near Kansas City, Missouri—is an example of a company using Web 2.0 dynamic content management technology to credibly showcase its ever-changing spectrum of new projects, and to enhance corporate brand awareness online. The company's site—OutpostWorldwide. net—is built on the enormously popular Wordpress (Wordpress.org) blog platform that is used by millions of bloggers around the world and by a growing number of corporate and news organizations, including *The New York Times*, *People Magazine* and eBay. The site gives visitors the ability to engage easily and openly in online comments, e-mail video and the company's news, share information to online social communities, and to subscribe to news update feeds that are delivered automatically through a service called FeedBurner (FeedBurner.com). FeedBurner, a company owned by Google, helps subscribers, like Outpost Worldwide, to optimize online awareness.

What's particularly attractive for the people at Outpost Worldwide is that the site can easily be updated from any computer that's online. There's no more dealing with complicated HTML Web design software when using Wordpress.

Web 2.0 and the multitude of new services and products it brings, like Wordpress, are revolutionizing how many organizations communicate with their employees, shareholders, customers, the media and partners through instantaneous sharing of information.

The CEO of an organization now has the ability, for example, to take the pulse of his or her company, engage employees in conversations directly, and get candid and unbiased feedback and ideas through personal internal blog conversations without filtering through divisional level managers. Leaders can use the communications technology of Web

2.0 to both speak and listen with greater clarity that ultimately will lead to better productivity, competitive advantages, and enhanced brand.

At Cisco Systems, Jeanette Gibson's job is to embrace and help define the future of online communications. It's also her passion, and few people I have spoken with see into the dynamic future of the exciting convergence of communications, information, and technology with greater clarity and leadership.

She is Director of New Media within Corporate Communications at Cisco Systems, a global company built on a culture of looking into the future of communication among people, communities, governments, and businesses worldwide.

With the Internet's openness and transparency and all of an organization's information out for the public to view, Gibson says, it's important to look at how you are viewed externally and whether that is the brand you want to showcase.

It's critical for executives to be involved in an organization's online strategy, Gibson says. At Cisco, for example, senior executives, including CEO John Chambers, are engaged with blogging and doing podcasts because they are finding that it helps them to better connect with audiences, trends, and immediate marketplace fluctuations. More important to the organization's image and reputation, these leaders give voice, face, and personality to a major corporation, and that equates to enhanced trust and connection with essential audiences.

It's inexpensive, she underscores, to roll out these tools of Web 2.0, and an executive need not be a technology expert to post and engage in personal online conversations with members of key audiences.

I asked Gibson to look into the future and share her advice to media savvy leaders on how to take charge of their own organization's online strategy, using the tools of Web 2.0:

- Consider your organization's culture. What is acceptable and what is your tolerance for risk? Any New Media program involves a sense of recognizing that you are no longer fully in control, a big challenge for many executives.

- Accept that we all are doing business in a new world. The landscape has changed. Doing business today requires a sense of transparency and new ways of engaging customers, employees, stakeholders, and other important audiences.

- Adapt technology to extend your distinct needs. Business-to-business, business-to-consumers, not-for-profits, government, NGOs ... customize online communications and the tools of Web 2.0 to achieve your own unique voice and brand image.

- Listen, watch, and monitor what's out there online about your organization. Recognize that what might be said about your organization on a social networking site, such as Facebook, might impact everything from recruiting new employees to brand image.

- Examine how your organization packages information. In the past, an organization might have just issued a press release. Today's communication trends require a careful look at messages, the kind of medium that can be used to enhance messages, how the information can be brought to life visually, and how online technology can be used to tell a more appealing story to a broader spectrum of audiences.

- Actively practice storytelling to bring your organization's messages and communications to life. For example, the headline of a Cisco news release read, "Cisco Gathers Global Leaders to Explore How Technology Can Transform Approach to Environmental Concerns, Sustainable, and Economic Development." The headline itself is captivating, positions the company as a leader, and is a readymade story that can be communicated effectively via nearly any tool of Web 2.0. For this event, the company's communications included a Webcast, blogging, podcasts, visuals, and corporate Web site support, together with the more traditional PR approaches.

Leadership online requires some risk. There is the reality of learning that not everyone loves your personality or your organization. But, there is also the direct chance of turning around a negative opinion and making a friend. Executive blogging requires time and attention each day in order to establish a conversation of credibility with audiences.

Even major public relations agencies have a lot to learn about the changing styles, dynamics, methods, and influence of the tools of Web 2.0; the smart ones are scrambling to learn.

Blogging and podcasting by leaders should not be delegated if you wish to achieve any level of trust and candor. An executive can never hope to build a dialogue by posting on a blog every couple of months. Blogging is a daily discipline of not only expressing opinion, but also of listening and establishing conversation.

Gibson underscores that the rise of social media and Web 2.0 is a strategic advantage for companies to better communicate, engage, collaborate, and respond to tomorrow's opportunities.

Knowledge of how to leverage and utilize the rapid convergence of communications, information, and Web 2.0 technologies will define tomorrow's leaders.

CHAPTER FOURTEEN

MANAGING CRISES THAT ATTRACT WORLD ATTENTION

Sometimes, a strategic communications assignment in support of an issue or cause is so immense, intricate, and controversial on a global scale that the only way to tackle it is to reach out for help among acquaintances in the media.

It was the spring of 2002, and emotions in America were still raw from the terrorist attacks of 9-11. The Bush administration had responded logically by sending troops to Afghanistan to seek out the proclaimed masterminds of the attacks, including Osama bin Laden, and ostensibly any of the other bad guys.

United States warplanes were bombing the country "back to the stone ages," administration pundits crowed. It was before the shift of attention to Iraq after bin Laden proved to be too difficult and too elusive to capture.

The White House had succeeded in convincing much of the country and many journalists that it was making the correct responses and those actions included herding up hundreds of possible "suspects" and incarcerating them.

Those men—whom Vice President Dick Cheney was calling "the worst of the worst" even before the U.S. knew anything about any of them—were first held in crowded detention stockades in Pakistan and Afghanistan. Many were stripped and beaten or sprayed for long times with cold water from hoses. Then, most were flown—stripped naked and hog-tied in inhuman positions on the cold bare metal floors of

U.S. cargo planes—to a newly cobbled together prison at the U.S. base of Guantánamo, on the island of Cuba, where they were held as enemy combatants.

The term, enemy combatants, had been concocted by the White House legal staff as a way to get around the law and to permit the U.S. to detain indefinitely anyone they did not like.

For all many of us knew, these so-called enemy combatants were some of the terrorists who had attacked our country on 9-11. The White House told us so.

What many of us did not fully comprehend at that time was that White House attorneys believed they had found a way to circumvent the Constitution, Bill of Rights, Geneva Convention, and all domestic and international laws pertaining to human rights and due process by using the enemy combatant label and through establishing a network of off-shore prisons that would give them freedom to hold and interrogate suspects for as long as they wanted. The administration wanted to block the suspects from access to attorneys, to their families, and to the outside world. Most of all, they wanted to prevent access to U.S. courts.

Early that April, I had a call from Thomas Wilner and Kristine Huskey, two prominent international human rights attorneys in Washington, D.C. They wanted to meet to discuss my potential help on a case they had just taken on—the plight of twelve Kuwaiti men believed to be detained at Guantánamo— and their plans to file a lawsuit against the Bush administration's intentions to deny the men of due process rights. The chairman of a public relations agency in Washington had referred me to Wilner and Huskey, saying his agency could not touch something so controversial, especially so soon after 9-11.

A day later, I was in their law offices on Pennsylvania Avenue that looked out at the United States Capitol. Wilner and Huskey said they had been hired through an intermediary law firm in Kuwait by the families of the Kuwaiti 12 to determine the fate of their loved ones. Wilner had sought out a communications strategist with connections to support planned litigation and to manage what he anticipated would become significant potential media interest. His instincts about media interest turned out to be accurate.

During the initial meeting, we identified a primary task: to draft several clear and accurate talking points or messages to help everyone involved speak as one voice, consistently from the same page.

We also agreed that the issue we were facing was not one of discussing or even speculating on the guilt or innocence of anyone because we knew so little about the 12 men. Besides that, guilt or innocence was irrelevant. The key issue and why I accepted the assignment was the denial of human rights and due process of law as afforded by the Constitution and the rule of law in our country.

Within a few days, I was on a flight to Kuwait to meet with the families—as Wilner and Huskey had done just a week earlier—and to try to piece together information about the 12 men so we could begin to get a picture of what we were facing. Upon my return, it was agreed that the three of us would compare notes.

During meetings with the family members in Kuwait—the fathers, mothers, children, wives, sons, daughters, and siblings—I intentionally and naturally fell into a journalist style of asking questions and then asking a similar question using different words to probe deeper for information, listen, and take copious notes.

I learned that many of the Kuwaitis had been captured not on any battlefield in or near Afghanistan, but rather in Pakistan while working individually on a variety of human rights efforts. It is a legacy among Kuwaitis, who are often more affluent than others in the Middle East, to assist with money and their own labor on agricultural projects and to build schools and mosques in neighboring regions.

For example, one detainee, Fouad Mahmoud Al Rabiah, was in his 40s, an aviation engineer with an established career at Kuwaiti Airlines and the father of four children. He had graduated from Embry-Riddle Aeronautical University and was granted honorary citizenship by the Daytona Beach, Florida, Chamber of Commerce. He had volunteered worked on a rescue campaign in Kosovo in 1988.

Another, Fayiz Mohammed Ahmed Al Kandari, was a university student who had traveled to Afghanistan during summer vacation prior to 9-11. It was his belief that helping others might honor his grandmother, who had just died, and bring better health to his mother, who is suffering from cancer.

Fawzi Khaled Al Odah was a school teacher in his 20s who had spent summers traveling in poor nations to educate less fortunate students. He had been caught in the turmoil in Pakistan after the extensive U.S. bombings and search for bin Laden in neighboring Afghanistan, and had simply been in the wrong place at the wrong time, swept up like many other men by U.S. forces because he looked out of place.

Fawzi was the son of my host in Kuwait, Khalid Al Odah. Khalid would become the international face and voice on behalf of the plight of the Kuwaiti detainees at Guantánamo and would eventually do hundreds of interviews over the years we worked together with journalists around the world.

Khalid loved America. He was a retired Kuwait Air Force colonel who had been trained by the United States Air Force in Arizona and had fought alongside U.S. forces in Operation Desert Storm in 1991. When we first met in April 2002, he was in a state of disbelief that the U.S. would be indiscriminately holding his son while making no attempt to determine his innocence.

At that time, in the spring of 2002, the U.S. had not yet gotten around to learning anything about the 12 Kuwaitis but rather just held them, along with about 600 other men, in Guantánamo in what increasingly appeared to be at least partly a PR stunt to reassure the American people that some of the bad people responsible for 9-11 were locked up.

It was better for those guys be in cells and under guard in a Guantánamo prison than to be bombing the streets of U.S. cities, according to the spin out of the White House and Pentagon, even though no one knew who they were or who was possibly innocent.

The story that attracted my attention during meetings in Kuwait and that I believed could potentially capture the media's interest, as well, were the reports—that were unconfirmed at that point—of bounty hunting and betrayal involving a U.S. operation that underscored the arbitrary nature of military sweeps to catch possible suspects.

During the intense and widespread bombing of Afghanistan in early 2002, U.S. forces were directed by the Pentagon to pay financial bounties to villagers in Pakistan near the Afghan border to betray any strangers they saw in the area.

American forces dropped leaflets that said, essentially, turn in a strange-looking Arab, get paid by the U.S. and feed your family for life.

It was not a strategic or incisive search for possible terrorists or even for bin Laden. Quite the contrary, U.S. forces were simply under orders to indiscriminately apprehend as many Arabs as possible. That is what the troops—young American men and women—were ordered to do. Their commanders said they were doing their part to catch bad guys.

Returning to Washington, Wilner, Huskey, and I regrouped, compared notes, and got to work. We framed a few talking points that would become the basis for media interviews:

- Just because our country was viciously attacked without warning is not justification to ignore our Constitution, Bill of Rights, and laws of our land.

- We are the world's symbol of freedom and should, as a nation, behave better than this. Yet, by creating an offshore prison to deny basic human rights is wrong and makes us no better than the worst.

- By denying access to due process of law, we are actually putting all Americans abroad, including our troops, in harm's way because we have disregarded the Geneva Convention rules on fair treatment.

Upon those few messages, written in plain language, powerful interviews were delivered with focus and clarity. Regardless of breaking news, our central talking points worked and endured over several years and hundreds of interviews.

The next challenge was to find someone in the media who might listen. Quite frankly, my concern was that no one might want to discuss the plight of some Kuwaitis held at Guantánamo because the Bush administration had worked to convince America that everyone held there was guilty of something.

My first call was to an old acquaintance at National Public Radio, Scott Simon, the popular, long-time anchor of NPR's Weekend Edition. Simon is widely respected for his integrity and strong sense of fairness. He suggested that I contact NPR's then-legal affairs correspondent Barbara Bradley Hagerty.

One call was all it took to get her attention. Hagerty's interest centered around the legal issue of arbitrary denial of due process of law to avoid certain rights afforded by the United States Constitution. She sensed correctly that it would become a big issue.

Over the next year, she reported numerous developments in the case of the 12 Kuwaitis, including a lengthy interview with Khalid Al-Odah.

While National Public Radio was open to balanced reporting on the Guantánamo situation, that wasn't the case at the *Washington Post*. After an initial meeting with a reporter resulted in a brief story on the Kuwaitis, the reporter quietly told us that his editors had prohibited further coverage on the subject. We were not surprised. *The Post* was one of several news organizations to be intimidated by the White House during those times and is even today struggling to regain its reputation as a meaningful news organization.

Aside from the courageous reporting on National Public Radio, not many journalists wanted to touch a story about detainees at Guantánamo. That all changed when Wilner, Huskey, and I met with Roy Gutman, then a correspondent at *Newsweek*.

Gutman had been awarded the 1993 Pulitzer Prize for stories revealing the horrors of ethnic warfare in the former Yugoslavia and was keenly interested in how a U.S. military sweep in Pakistan after 9-11 based on bounty and betrayal had led to the indiscriminate capture of several of the Kuwaiti detainees.

Working with *Newsweek* staff in Pakistan, Gutman confirmed the U.S. Arab-for-bounty program and even got his hands on several of the leaflets that promised enough money to feed a family for life in exchange for turning in an Arab. His team of reporters also confirmed early reports of prisoner mistreatment by U.S. troops.

Gutman's extensive cover story dominated an issue of *Newsweek* in the early summer of 2002 and contributed significantly to raising questions about the propriety of U.S. actions with regard to Guantánamo.

Between Gutman's piece in Newsweek and Bradley Hagerty's continued coverage on National Public Radio, the tide shifted dramatically throughout the news media. All of a sudden, reporters were calling from around the country and from news organizations around the world.

Coverage of the plight of the 12 Kuwaitis that were held

incommunicado at Guantánamo became widespread—Associated Press, BBC News, *Newark Star-Ledger*, CBS 60 Minutes, Agence France-Presse, CNN, ABC World News Tonight, CBS Evening News, *Orlando Sentinel, Miami Herald*, the *New York Times, International Herald Tribune*—and on and on, except the *Washington Post*.

Journalists were interested in both the human rights angle and new developments as the legal team of Wilner and Huskey argued the case through the federal courts on the way to the United States Supreme Court.

When we were contacted by reporters who were new to the story, they generally wanted to know what other respected journalists had written about the Kuwaiti detainees.

We actively used a Web site, KuwaitiDetainees.org, to bring together background information about the Kuwaiti 12, photos, court documents, and hyperlinks to all of the media coverage and dozens of stories.

When reporters want to tackle a story with a sometimes edgy angle, like that of the Kuwaiti detainees, it is helpful for them to have a way to easily point to what other news organizations have reported on the subject when getting clearance from their editors to proceed. The Web site—which we got online within two days—worked perfectly to validate the importance of our story among a growing corps of journalists worldwide.

Content on KuwaitiDetainees.org changed each day with fresh updates and extensive background information on the legal case, including copies of legal briefs, plus background and photos of the Kuwaiti detainees, contact information to help journalists reach us at anytime of the day or night, and the growing number of hyperlinks to the extensive media coverage, listed by news organization and date. Traffic to the site soared.

Within a few months, nearly every meaningful news organization in the world had reported the story about the 12 Kuwaiti detainees at Guantánamo. Perhaps even more important, coverage of the whole issue of unjust imprisonment of hundreds of men and denial of human rights by U.S. policy and actions at Guantánamo had become a global story.

I wish I could end this story on a happy note and report that that our team helped to achieve the expeditious release of the 12 men. I wish

I could share with you that we were successful—that all the lawsuits and news coverage had worked—not to mention the staggering emotional and financial burden the detentions caused for the families in Kuwait.

Yet, even after more than five years of incarceration at Guantánamo, Vice President Cheney is still out making fund-raising speeches before wealthy Republicans, claiming that the people at Guantánamo are "the worst of the worst" terrorists even though no charges were ever filed.

In the end, the Bush administration was slow to release innocent people from Guantánamo—America's embarrassing "black hole"—and none of the Kuwaiti 12 was ever charged with any crime or wrongdoing.

Let me share another example of responsibly managed communications during an event that still echoes in our memories.

Sometimes, all the advance planning in the world cannot begin to address how to manage communications when the unthinkable happens. But advance planning helps.

In the aftermath of the worst and most horrific handgun-killing spree in America's history, there was considerable second-guessing about the crisis communications of Virginia Tech in Blacksburg, Virginia, specifically over how the university warned students and faculty about the dangers of that day.

Critics, led by many people in the news media and by a handful of others with something to sell, voiced sharp criticism that the university had not done enough during a two-hour gap between the first shooting of a young woman in a dormitory and the subsequent indiscriminant mass murders of 31 more students and teachers across campus in a lecture hall on Monday, April 16, 2007.

The next morning, Virginia Tech President Charles W. Steger was interviewed by NBC's Matt Lauer on the "Today" show. Lauer repeatedly pushed for an explanation why the university had not "locked down" (a prison term that is unfortunately applied to our schools) the entire campus and whether the university could have done a better job of alerting people on campus to the threats. Despite the badgering, Steger stuck to clear, logical, and consistent messages.

Steger explained to Lauer that with more than 26,000 students, Virginia Tech has the population of many towns, and, consequently, it would not be responsible to impulsively overreact without knowing all the facts. While acknowledging the two-hour gap, he emphasized that the university had, indeed, sent out an alert across the university via e-mail, voicemail, the campus public address system, and the university's Web site.

Steger gave an exceptional interview to the talk show host who didn't quite seem to comprehend the situation and was apparently hung up on a preconceived notion about what he thought the story should be, regardless of the realities. As we have seen so many times in the past, such approaches by some news people, while often not grounded in fact, are commonplace in today's media environment.

By any standard, Virginia Tech's responsiveness to a tragedy of unimaginable scope was exemplary and should set new standards for clear and concise crisis communications, especially using many of the tools of New Media online.

By late morning on Monday, April 16, Virginia Tech's Web site was being updated constantly with information, alerts, directions, and resources. The university had posted the first of what would be the first of many podcasts of statements from officials, including Tech's president, Charles W. Steger.

Within just a few hours, the university had taken charge of its communications and was speaking with a clear and consistent voice. Even before the deeply sorrowful task of identifying the dead, those few early updates that the university made were immediately communicated to the students, faculty, parents, Blacksburg community, and the world. There was no speculation, just facts.

At the same time, Virginia Tech's site had been changed completely to reflect the gravity of events. The university's normal site was gone and a new site provided even more information, often updated every few minutes, about news, memorials, and events.

The site—which reflected simplicity and clarity—had been divided into three sections: at the top, a series of remarkable photographs with quotes from leaders; at the bottom, one section labeled "The Latest;" and a third, the heading, "Resources/Related Content." In the latter, there was a new section, among many, that guided students and faculty to grief counseling services.

This was not a stereotypical example of a "dark site" brought to life, as some PR agencies like to promote to clients. VT-dot-edu was new in response to a crisis of unbelievable proportions and reflected the impact of what had happened while responsibly providing information leadership to the university community. Most of all, it was credible.

By clicking on a link, you were taken to the site's "back-end" that was using blog and HTML technology for instantaneous updates by multiple people. There were transcripts and streaming audio and video, and, yes, you could find elements of the university's normal site. It is unprecedented in the history of crisis communications on the Internet.

Here's the important part: It was all being done within the university by a team of faculty and administrators working around the clock and somehow finding the inner strength to manage their grief and emotions with a commitment to communicate accurately with the world.

Soon after the Virginia Tech shootings, I spoke with Larry Hincker, who leads university relations, and Michael Dame, the university's director of Web communications. Both remained at the epicenter of all communications by Virginia Tech during the crisis.

Hincker has been connected with the university much of his adult life. He was a student there, then worked in corporate communications at a utility company and Rockwell before returning to Virginia Tech in the late 1980s.

"I believe in this notion of building a strong internal team," he told me. "I try to give people who work for me as much space as possible ... you give people authority and responsibility to grow, and then when a crisis comes they intrinsically know what to do."

"One of the reasons we were able to do what we did (in communications during the shooting crisis) was that we didn't have corporate lawyers breathing down our neck. Our university counsel (Kay Heidbreder) said, 'we don't have a legal problem here, we have a PR challenge,'" Hincker shared.

And, once again, there was that recurring confirmation of the trend in leadership in contemporary communications—develop the expertise you need in-house rather than rely on an outside agency. In fact, during the Virginia Tech crisis, no PR agency even extended a hand of assistance to the university until nearly a week later.

I asked Hincker to what extent he had developed an advance

communications crisis plan, and he replied that he had two versions—
one in the required university official format and one which was his
own. The latter approached crisis communications on a more realistic
and practical level: It focused on training, assigned clear areas of
responsibility, and used solid experience.

Did he reach for the crisis plan, I asked? "Hell, no … I didn't
reach for any damn book," was his answer. "We were operating 100
percent on instinct, things were happening so fast. We were dealing
with multiple news updates online as dozens of satellite trucks started
rolling up on campus, and we had our first press conference at noon.

"We played it straight, and that kind of openness was disarming
… which was helpful in the way the media covered us."

Dame was a critical member of Hincker's communications team
and responsible for everything online. He was a veteran journalist
with more than 20 years in the news business before joining Virginia
Tech a year prior to the shootings. He had run the online news site at
the *Orlando Sentinel* for many years so he was knowledgeable of the
dynamics of fast-breaking news and crisis situations, such as hurricanes.
I was not surprised to find him to be a seasoned professional who
anticipated and handled such emergencies proficiently.

Dame's insider story of the details of handling a major crisis
is an important learning experience for anyone responsible for
communications in today's digital revolution.

"As soon as I heard about the first shooting," Dame told me, "I
started thinking, 'What do we need to do if this escalates?'"

"We have a light version of our home page—some people call it
"dark" site. But that implies you have an entire Web site ready to go.
Ours is actually a stripped down home page void of Flash, photos, and
heavy graphics. It's just text. At the top is a header that reads, "Campus
Alert." Under that is the alert information. We have that template ready
to go. We just have to prepare the message and get it online.

"So I got with my staff and said, 'If we need to switch over to
this and take down Flash—be ready.' We also talked to IT regarding
potential server overload. So, basically, everyone went into crisis
preparation mode.

"We first posted up the light version of our home page. Second,
we started pulling down flash and graphics from the home page. Three,

we took steps to shut down the 'VT News' database to improve server performance.

"The only news you could find was about the shooting itself. All of our resources were dedicated to providing news and information tied only to this event. You couldn't even access our database of normal news or things like calendar events. So those were the key steps: go with the light version, shut down the database, and add server capacity.

"There's no way we could have had a plan for a massacre. We did have a crisis plan and all those steps were taken—but the magnitude of this tragedy was unprecedented. Our job is to plan for unexpected or unimaginable. But how can you plan for that? How can you foresee something like this?"

What about the media's push for blame, I asked him, particularly over the so-called two-hour gap when some journalists had suggested the university could have done more? This was Dame's response:

"Having been in media for 20 years, I can say they were doing their jobs. If I were in that situation, I would have done the same. They were just trying to get to the facts. Assigning blame—that's part of the culture of cable news today. As soon as something happens, the pundits want to assign blame or give credit before they get all facts. Cable news is a game—it's all about ratings and keeping viewers glued to the channel. So they sensationalize to do that. We're not the only group who has experienced that.

"The punditry on cable news taking the place of real news—that was frustrating. The pundits were dishing out opinions and not just the facts. They just confused viewers and fed the rumor mill. That's cable news today for you, unless you watch CNN Headline News. That's the only legitimate cable 'news.' FOX and even the CNN parent station are all half punditry, half news.

"It is the style of today's 24/7 news cycle," Dame told me. "The news channels live for this type of event."

"So, what did you and the others who are responsible for communications at Virginia Tech learn?" I asked. The words that Mike Dame used, well, I suggest that they be read over and over to be considered and discussed by anyone who is responsible for reputation management of an organization:

"Having a 'brand' or image that is strong even during crises starts with your values and mission. It's all about who you are as an organization—not the specific wording you use in a press release or announcement or update, for example.

"You have to work hard to make your values and mission a living part of your culture. It's beyond words and more about behavior. We've been lucky to have had that here for decades.

"For companies, it's much more difficult. But start at the top analyzing what you're really about. Then codify it. Then your people need to live that mission. That's an internal communications role more than a media relations one, I think. Establishing a kind of consistency behind that mission and culture can be tough for PR people, particularly when you consider that PR people hop job to job and company to company a lot. How can you develop a culture that sticks with 30 to 40 percent turnover? At the university level, it's easier because professors get tenure, students (at Virginia Tech) are Hokies for life, and staff tends to stay around longer than they would at, say, an agency.

"So I guess my take away lesson on this is that it's all about inculcating your mission and values into your culture. You can't just do that with messaging. You can't script people or coach them to say the right things. Memorizing talking points isn't living the message. What you have seen and heard … is all about who we are. It's not about scripted message points. It's real," said Dame.

Several months after the shootings at Virginia Tech, I went back to Hincker to ask what lessons may be learned from crisis communications during that horrific event.

Here is what he said, "One walks a fine line between openness and responsiveness on one hand, and on the other hand, just not engaging when necessary. We have tried to continue with a rather wide open approach on even the most delicate topics … I am of the opinion that in the public sector there are no secrets.

"I think our colleagues in the media appreciate that openness, and while I don't expect that they will write favorably on every topic, it (openness) does help reduce what might otherwise be an 'edge' in some stories."

The powerful spirit of Virginia Tech lives on today, months after the murders of April 16, 2007. Being a Hokie has always been a source of deep pride for the university's students. Now, however, others of us have come to know, admire, and honor that spirit—the university's brand—in part because of the honesty we heard from Tech during its darkest time in history.

Here in northern Virginia as I write, a VT flag still hangs from the balcony of a neighbor's home, months later. Students at nearby George Mason University in Fairfax, Virginia, adorned the statue of their school's founder in the maroon and orange colors of Virginia Tech as a tribute.

The sadness of the murders at Virginia Tech have touched and changed the lives of many people. Hincker is no exception.

"I live this everyday and work on nothing but post-April 16 duties. It is disheartening and sad because we had really great momentum going on a lot of projects which today I see out there on the horizon awaiting my attention."

With the experience of years both as a journalist and in strategic communications worldwide, I have never before witnessed an organization communicate more effectively during a tragedy and crisis of such scale than Virginia Tech. What struck me most was how the leadership of the university managed to respond so quickly and in such an efficient and credible manner at a time when shock and grief tended to be overwhelming.

It is important to note that all of the advance crisis planning, as well as all management of events, at the university in southwestern Virginia during that dark week in April, was handled by an internal university team of staff and faculty. The crisis planning began years before, after the events in New York, Washington, and Pennsylvania on 9-11-01. Virginia's state assembly helped in preparation by mandating crisis plans at all schools in the Commonwealth.

The Virginia Tech communications staff had a solid, practical, and realistic working plan, including delegation of responsibility, when a horrific event happened on campus, and the whole university has benefited as a result. No public relations or crisis communications agencies were involved. Virginia Tech's in-house team of professionals was in place, trained, and knew what needed to be done.

CHAPTER FIFTEEN

A MORE PLIABLE AND
BUYABLE NEW MEDIA

Changes within the business of news worldwide together with the dawning of New Media have raised questions about what is journalism today and who is a journalist. When many people think of New Media, they often think of bloggers, interactive Web sites, and Internet-related news and opinion sources.

Wikipedia says New Media is, "a broad term that usually refers to new technologies and communication methods in the context of their effects on the established mainstream news media." Clearly, New Media is evolving in its definition and is one of those big basket or *superset* terms that includes many forms of interactive communications using technology.

In the public relations industry, some agencies have often turned to the self-styled reporters of New Media after having had chronically disappointing results when attempting to pitch stories to the mainstream or traditional media. But, the efforts are sometimes overshadowed by controversy.

When Microsoft launched its new Vista personal computer operating system, working with the Edelman public relations agency, one of their tactics raised questions about what is the legitimate news media and what is not.

Bloggers are not for the most part considered the legitimate news media and, consequently, generally not held accountable to the same standards of conduct and training as *real* journalists. Yet, the fallout from the Microsoft Vista PC promotion suggested that some in the public relations industry were attempting to invent a more pliable and buyable media through New Media.

The Edelman campaign to promote Microsoft's Vista operating system intended to get bloggers talking about the technical aspects of the software. The agency chose 90 bloggers and used several versions of an e-mail—apparently in pecking order of perceived importance— to ask them if they wanted to receive an Acer Ferrari laptop, valued at $2,200, loaded with the new Vista software to review, no strings attached.

Here is the exact Microsoft e-mail signed by the company that was sent to one blogger who writes about the software industry and accepted the Vista PC gift:

> *I enjoy your blog. I'm working on getting some hardware out to key community folks, and I'd like to offer you a review PC. I'd love to send you a loaded Ferrari 1000 courtesy of Windows Vista and AMD. Are you interested?*
>
> *This would be a review machine, so I'd love to hear your opinion on the machine and OS. Full disclosure— while I hope you will tell others about your experience with the pc, you don't have to. Also, you are welcome to send the machine back to us after you are done playing with it, or you can give it away on your site, or you can keep it. My recommendation is that you give it away on your site, but it's your call. Just let me know your opinion on Windows Vista and what you plan to do with it when the time comes.*
>
> *If you are game, would you send me your address and phone?*

Straight-forward and direct. The blogger could accept the freebee or say no. Nearly all said yes.

Rick Murray, president of Edelman's Me2Revolution, said the firm covered all disclosure bases, and it appears they had, but by their own rules.

Any responsible journalist or anyone who considered himself to be a journalist would have declined because the gift compromises long-established and certainly well-known rules of ethics in the news media profession.

I asked Walt Mossberg of the *Wall Street Journal* —perhaps the most influential and respected journalist who covers technology in America—for his thoughts about the Vista giveaway and whether he had been approached.

"No, I wasn't offered one and would of course never have accepted it," Mossberg replied. "I do borrow equipment for review from various companies, but I return it all. It is flatly unethical for any journalist, including a blogger, to accept and keep a laptop. In general, with big items like computers, the offer of a loan (again, a short-term loan, not a gift) is made before anything is sent, or the reviewer asks."

The Microsoft Vista and computer gift targeted bloggers and curiously not top opinion-leaders in the mainstream news media. If the intent was to create buzz and mindshare in the tech industry, it was mission accomplished. But, at what cost to Microsoft's reputation and to Vista given the fallout?

Maria Aspan wrote in the *New York Times*, "the gifts generated controversy as well as goodwill, as many in that (tech) community accused Microsoft of bribery and their peers of unethical behavior."

A closer look at the hue and cry among bloggers revealed another dramatic difference from legitimate journalists. The uproar was coming mostly from bloggers whining that they were not included among the favored 90 who received the free laptops. Reading their blogs, the comments left the impression of being immature and unprofessional. But then, these are bloggers who use their online sites to espouse personal opinions, including bias, not unlike those who stand on a soapbox and shout whatever comes into their mind at Speakers' Corner at Hyde Park in London.

The larger question of greater concern is whether some PR people—using gimmicks such as the Vista PC giveaway—are attempting to create their own brand of media coverage by influencing more susceptible bloggers as an alternative to more meaningful and potentially substantive outreach on behalf of clients by working with the mainstream news media.

CHAPTER SIXTEEN

IT'S THE "MEDIA"

Media. At first blush you may think this is not a big deal or just nitpicking terminology. You may be right. Then again, perhaps not.

The difference between *press* and *media* is subtle but important. Understanding the difference is important if you are to be effective in strategic communications. At the very least, it shows you are savvy about the news media.

The term *press* originated from the printing press and has been associated with the newspaper business for decades. A caricature of the press evolved in black and white motion pictures years ago of reporters with large "press" cards stuck in the brims of their hats, sometimes lugging big cameras that fired off golf ball-sized flash bulbs. Those days are over and gone.

Nonetheless, hundreds of Web sites for organizations large and small still refer visitors to their "press room." Such use of the word screams at site visitors that this is an organization that is, well, not keeping up with the times. Incidentally, a press room is where the printing presses are located to physically print a paper.

To many journalists, your knowledge of the difference between press and media quietly says something about you and your level of knowledge and awareness in working with today's media. I've known some broadcast reporters who were offended when someone called them the press. They are not, so why call them that? It may not be a deal breaker as to whether they do a story, but it's the sort of thing that can get you off on the wrong foot with a reporter. You may never know what a broadcast newsperson or any journalist thinks about being called the press. Play it safe and professional.

Now you may be thinking, "Hey, wait a minute, Henderson. I hear reporters using the word *press* and *press release* all the time. What gives?!"

Well, it's their industry, and they can call it and themselves whatever they wish. My point is that in this era of 24-hour cable news programs, up-to-the-minute Internet news services, split-second news cycles, emerging technology, and rapidly changing methods of instantly reporting the news from virtually anywhere on earth, the term *press* is passé and about as old-fashioned as an old typewriter. Heck, even the definition of *reporter* is up for grabs these days now that video taken on your cell phone might air on a television newscast. You might be a tax attorney one minute, take history-making video on your phone the next, and end up being called a citizen journalist by the end of the day. So let's try to be as clear as possible.

If we are going to do an effective job at reaching out to get the media's attention in this fast-changing environment, let's work to set the pace. Using old terminology is neither hip nor cool and just might be a turnoff to a twenty-something blogger out there who is creating tomorrow's world of journalism.

News media, or simply the *media*, refers to the organizations and the people who cover, report, edit, direct, and produce the news, whether for television, radio, newspapers, magazines, blogs, or the evolving use of the Internet for communication of information.

Today's journalists and bloggers are members of the media, not necessarily the press.

CHAPTER SEVENTEEN

ONE SIZE DOES NOT FIT ALL

It wasn't that long ago that newspaper editors and broadcast news producers sat in ivory towers and ran stories that they believed their broad audiences would need to know about. Those were the days—before government deregulation and all of today's choices for news—when we dutifully sat down each evening, usually in our living rooms, to watch the 30-minute newscasts of ABC, NBC, and CBS.

In many communities across the country, this was how Americans learned what happened in the world that day—or at least what the news decision makers in New York thought we should know.

There's the legendary story that on the day that the Three Mile Island nuclear reactor nearly melted down in March 1979 in Pennsylvania, CBS Evening News chose to lead with a story about Britain's Queen Elizabeth because the producers in New York thought that, in the realm of world events, the queen was a more important story. They were wrong.

Today nobody remembers the story about the queen, but a lot of people still remember Three Mile Island.

It was a pivotal moment—a wake-up call—for CBS News. Viewers and affiliate stations alike responded that the news division was out of touch with its audience, and it was.

Most media decision makers today are keenly aware of who their primary audiences are and what kind of news is most likely to appeal to them. The news business today is formula-driven to satisfy the perceived news and interest appetites of specific groups and demographics.

It's not only "All The News That's Fit To Print," as the *New York Times* says. It's also the news that you are likely to be interested in and talk about with your friends and colleagues. That's how popular newspapers and broadcast news programs become even more successful: by focusing on stories that appeal to audiences. The purpose of journalism now is to sell newspapers and magazines and build audiences for broadcast stations, networks, and cable channels.

The kind of story, for example, that runs on the front page of one daily newspaper might not appeal to editors at another newspaper in the same city. For all kinds of reasons—political, cultural, economic, demographic, and/or social—each media outlet has its own primary target audiences.

USA Today, for example, has a style geared to business people on the run, with incisively written and very timely stories encapsulated in as few words as possible. *USA Today* wants to make sure you learned about it first from them.

Its detractors have called *USA Today* "the McPaper" because, like fast food, you can consume it quickly and there is little nourishment or depth. Some of the paper's features amount to little more than nuggets of information that editors believe their readers want. But *USA Today* has been highly successful for over two decades, because it knows and focuses on specific audiences.

USA Today has essentially reinvented the way news is presented today, using crisp color and concise editorial content, graphics, and visuals. The paper has forced other media decision makers to rethink their broad marketing appeal and re-evaluate how they fit on the competitive landscape in order to stay in business.

It's not surprising that the type of in-depth and sometimes lengthy news analysis you find in the *New York Times* won't appear in *USA Today*. Both newspapers are popular, well-written, and respected, yet each has an entirely different approach to covering news. Each has its own primary audience. So while any news organization—whether newspaper or broadcast or magazine or online—wants to capture the largest audience possible, they have carefully defined primary audiences, and they work hard to feel the pulse of those audiences.

Today's effective media-conscious executive or strategic communications professional must also have his or her finger on that pulse, evaluating the journalistic trends and even the politics of several different news organizations in order to find the right home for a favorable story. A story that would be perfect for National Public Radio might be dismissed by the more conservative Fox News.

Beyond the more traditional news media is today's 24-hour news cycle and the instant reach of Internet news sites and news-oriented blogs. We live in the age of instant news coverage, when a story carried on the Associated Press wire in America can appear on the Web site of a newspaper in Melbourne, Australia, in the blink of an eye.

So, in communicating a message through the media, how do you find the best place for your story?

- *Target.* Make a list of communities or cities or places where you want news of your organization to appear. Include trade magazines and think about whether your story might cross over and appeal to trades in more than one industry sector. Call it your "shopping list" because, as when we go to the mall, sometimes our shopping list is a little grander than our budget.

- *Get smart.* Read up on specific publications and news outlets on your shopping list. Have they covered your type of story before? What are their political influences or overtones? What are the general demographics of their audience? What sort of depth might they devote to a story about your organization? Believe it or not, the *National Inquirer* may be a terrific way to reach an enormous audience segment with a consumer-oriented story that might not appeal to editors at the *Los Angeles Times.*

- *Shoot high.* Just because *The Wall Street Journal* has never before reported on your industry sector doesn't mean they are not interested in your company.

As head of corporate communications at Gulfstream Aerospace, I found that while most business reporters hadn't been interested for years in a stereotypical story pitch about the merits of business aircraft, they were attracted to a skillfully crafted story pitch about the hot new trend among corporations of buying ultra-expensive, ultra-long-range business jets.

When I invited select groups of top-level mainstream journalists from around the world to experience a flight aboard the $40-million Gulfstream V at 50,000 feet, far above all other aircraft traffic, and at a speed faster than most commercial airliners, it always guaranteed a great story, sometimes on the front page. They always mentioned one of our key selling points: The Gulfstream V is the world's longest range, high performance business jet. The same story angle about the Gulfstream V appeared in every major publication and television news outlet around the world, and during that time, orders for the new aircraft increased 443 percent.

In today's style of strategic communications, part of the trick to capturing a reporter's attention is to begin by identifying the right media outlet for your story, with keen attention paid to placement opportunities at online news sites and news-oriented blogs.

CHAPTER EIGHTEEN

BE FRIENDLY, BE FUNNY, AND BE HONEST

We are in a new era for both the news media and for people who want to communicate through the media … and there are high hopes on both sides.

In recent years, the news media has been faced with its own concerns over credibility. The industry has suffered more than its share of figurative black eyes. There have been revelations of reporters making up stories, fabricating details, and reporting interviews that never took place, sometimes with imaginary people.

There are many examples.

A reporter named Janet Cooke at the *Washington Post* won a Pulitzer Prize for a story about an 8-year-old heroin addict. It was subsequently revealed that there was no such person. Cooke resigned from the paper and was stripped of the Pulitzer.

At the venerable *New York Times*, it was discovered that Jayson Blair, a rising star in the newsroom, had made up dozens of stories, sometimes plagiarizing the work of other reporters, or just downright lying in his writing.

The reputation of CBS News was shaken to the core when anchorman Dan Rather broadcast allegations on the program "60 Minutes II" about George Bush's National Guard service 30 years earlier. It turned out that Rather's report, which aired during the 2004 presidential campaign, was based on documents of unsubstantiated and questionable origin. Faced with intense criticism from the White

House and conservative bloggers as well as several investigations, Rather announced within a month that he would step down as anchorman of the CBS Evening News. CBS's "60 Minutes II" was canceled soon after.

Fallout from the intense and loud criticism from a small but well-orchestrated ultra-conservative group that supported President George W. Bush's re-election efforts sent ripples of fear through the news media at a time during the hot presidential race when some news organizations were looking into reports of ballot-box tampering and other irregularities. The media became "gun shy," as one journalist told me, of further investigative reporting. It may well have been that by going after Dan Rather over a story that was fundamentally true but based on unverified documents, conservative groups managed to not only control but also manipulate the news media from covering an even larger story.

Then there was Stephen Glass, who admitted making up sources and whole news stories while a staff reporter for *The New Republic* magazine.

The technology bubble of the late 1990s was also a sobering experience for the media. Many reporters were sucked into the hype and convinced by the overblown claims of tech's high flyers. There was fierce competition between news organizations to report the latest tech industry developments, even when they lacked substance and validation. In the end, most if not all of the claims turned out to be nothing more than hot air.

The irresponsible or unwise actions of a few people in the media have at times injured the reputations of otherwise outstanding and conscientious news organizations.

In most cases, respected news organizations acted quickly to understand what went wrong with their internal standards of checks and balances and took corrective action. So what we have today is a news media that has expeditiously conducted a responsible job of re-examination and is keenly aware of its responsibility as the guardians of fair, accurate, responsible, and balanced reporting. Traditional news organizations must regain audience trust. Consequently the transparency of news organizations as they go about their trade of journalism is a growing trend.

The *New York Times,* for instance, hired Byron Calame, a journalist from the more conservative *Wall Street Journal,* as its people editor. His role is advocate for the paper's readers—the crucial audience often ignored in newsgathering.

Calame regularly takes an unbiased look at questions of fairness and accuracy in the *Times* and freely reports his conclusions on the paper's Sunday op-ed page. His reports are unvarnished. It is not uncommon for him to write that the paper made a mistake on a story. He has even taken reporters and editors to task over their handling of a story.

In one case, Calame wrote, "One of the real tests of journalistic integrity is being fair to someone who might be best described by a four-letter word. The *New York Times* flunked such a test in rejecting a demand by Geraldo Rivera of Fox News for a correction of a sentence about him in a column by the paper's chief television critic."

Calame also has a blog to focus on matters that aren't appropriate for his column in the Sunday op-ed pages or won't fit into them. His direct telephone number, e-mail, and mailing addresses are all included for easy access by readers.

He and the *Times* have recognized that the future of the news industry is participatory journalism, defined by the Media Center at the American Press Institute as "the act of a citizen, or group of citizens, playing an active role in the process of collecting, reporting, analyzing, and disseminating news and information."

Many other news organizations have beefed up editorial scrutiny of stories and fact-checking as best they can within budget constraints and staffing cutbacks. Internally, questions are asked if a story seems too dramatic, too bold, too cutting-edge. Outwardly, the media has learned to smell hype coming their way from several miles away and avoid it like the plague.

Therein lies a basic challenge of strategic communications today: how to credibly communicate what your organization wants to say to its public audiences or stakeholders via the media while, at the same time, understanding the ever-changing and often trendy needs and methods of the news business. Methods that seemed to work last month may not achieve any results today.

Strategic communications requires persistence and fresh

approaches. It certainly is not in any organization's best interest to adopt an attitude toward the media that might be perceived as arrogant or pushy.

Veteran Washington, D.C., reporter Lyle Denniston said, "A 'savior of the world' or 'working for the good of all of us' complex is always unconvincing. I am never persuaded that, as General Motors goes, so goes the nation.

"The competition of conflicting private interests reflects the openness of American society. As a journalist, however, I say just tell me what you're up to; you do not need to assume that I agree with your agenda in order to expect me to treat it with professional respect."

Many journalists simply are skeptical of public relations people, perhaps fearing hidden agendas. "PR people need to be less controlling and manipulative," said veteran ABC and CBS network television correspondent John Laurence.

In many ways, communications with the news media mirrors behavior. An organization that dodges facts and manipulates issues will ultimately erode whatever credibility it may have. On the other hand, a leading organization in any given industry will be identified by how well it communicates with the media in an open, candid, and professional manner.

Arthur Page, vice president of public relations at AT&T for two decades and the public relations professional after whom the Arthur W. Page Society was named, wrote, "All business in a democratic country begins with public permission and exists by public approval."

Page viewed public relations as the art of developing, understanding, and communicating character—both corporate and individual.

This vision, albeit somewhat halcyon by nature in today's world, was an outgrowth of Page's belief in humanism and freedom as America's guiding characteristics and as preconditions for capitalism.

Whenever I hear an organization talk about best practices, I am reminded of Page's statements on corporate behavior and the role of public relations. Best practices for many corporations and not-for-profit groups has too often become an elaborate exercise in developing flowery rhetoric and, in the end, fairly unimaginative and empty proclamations that some executives recite with what can only be described as a divine glow, as if the tone of their voice will make the declarations sound deeper than they are. What Page said, by sharp contrast, is clear and pragmatic and remains rock solid to this day.

Page believed idealistically that the successful organization must shape its character in concert with that of the nation. It must operate in the public interest, manage for the long term, and make customer satisfaction its primary goal.

"Real success, both for big business and the public," Page said, "lies in large enterprise conducting itself in the public interest and in such a way that the public will give it succinct freedom to serve effectively."

Page viewed media relations as the art of developing, understanding, and communicating corporate and individual character, and he practiced seven principles of public relations management as a means of implementing his philosophy.

Today the seven Page Principles that help to define integrity in media relations are deceptively simple:

1. *Tell the truth.* Let the public know what's happening, and provide an accurate picture of the company's character, ideals, and practices.

2. *Prove it with action.* Public perception of an organization is determined 90 percent by what it does and 10 percent by talking.

3. *Listen to the customer.* To serve the company well, understand what the public wants and needs. Keep top decision makers and other employees informed about public reaction to company products, policies, and practices.

4. *Manage for tomorrow.* Anticipate public reaction and eliminate practices that create difficulties. Generate goodwill.

5. *Realize a company's true character is expressed by its people.* The strongest opinions—good or bad—about a company are shaped by the words and deeds of its employees. As a result, every employee—active or retired—is involved with public relations. It is the responsibility of corporate

communications to support each employee's capability and desire to be an honest, knowledgeable ambassador to customers, friends, shareowners, and public officials.

6. *Conduct public relations as if the whole company depends on it.* Corporate relations is a management function. No corporate strategy should be implemented without considering its impact on the public. The public relations professional is a policymaker capable of handling a wide range of corporate communications activities.

7. *Remain calm, patient, and good-humored.* Lay the groundwork for public relations miracles with consistent, calm and reasoned attention to information and contacts. When a crisis arises, remember that cool heads communicate best.

Linda Stasi, longtime columnist for the *New York Post*, candidly sums it up this way: "Be honest, be friendly, and be funny. The best PR people are people who are honest, and in many, many cases are people who have become my friends."

Honesty and integrity are qualities that leaders and those responsible for working directly with the media need to own and communicate tirelessly throughout their organizations, through words and deeds. Effective strategic communications begins with words as well as actions that are accurate, comprehensive, and formed by integrity.

CHAPTER NINETEEN

HERE COME THE LEMMINGS

Ever wonder why so many stories you first read in this morning's paper show up later on the evening television newscast with little or no update? And have you ever wondered why that interesting story you heard on National Public Radio a couple of weeks ago is just now making it into the newspaper?

There exists a pecking order in America's news media. Let's draw an analogy to the much-maligned Alaskan lemming, the rodent creature that, according to popular myth, runs in packs, first in one direction and then the other, seemingly without rhyme or reason—even if headed over a cliff. Ah, but there is rhyme and reason in the news media. There are some in the pack more trusted than others.

Despite all the appearances of competition between America's print and broadcast news media, what is covered by the news media and the style in which it is covered is largely influenced by how someone else in the news media has previously reported the story. For lack of a better description, let's call this the *lemming effect*. It's all about leadership—and, perhaps, lack of it—and a hierarchy of influence within the news media.

This effect shows up most often in the area of enterprise news reporting—the side of journalism that requires digging for unusual angles, finding outstanding sources, and unearthing award-winning stories. Enterprise stories are generally found first on National Public Radio news programs or on the pages of major daily newspapers. Television news, in most cases, has accepted the default job of reporting the follow-up on the original story—and making it as sensational as possible, often to give the impression that they came up with the story even though they did not.

Here's how it works: Even though television news has been around a half a century and is perhaps the most powerful of the news media, the decision makers of TV news are an insecure group. With few exceptions, they will not consider running any story that smacks of controversy until it has appeared first in print, either in a newspaper or on a wire service.

One motivator for this approach is an unspoken fear that a story might upset an advertiser. Advertisers rule. News coverage rolls over.

At the morning story planning sessions at each of the television networks in New York, producers sit around the room with copies of that day's *New York Times* in their laps. What appears in the morning *Times* often influences what America will see nine hours later on the evening television news.

It is no different in local television newsrooms in communities around the country. What will appear on the evening news is influenced by that morning's local newspaper. And stories that appeared overnight on the Associated Press broadcast wire service often provide ideas for local coverage later that day. Consequently, much of what viewers see at the end of the day is recycled old news, often from the day before.

Sure, there are exceptions, such as breaking news. The network news operations have wars, natural disasters, and news conferences to cover during the day. Local news covers fires, car wrecks, and local news conferences. But even then television news is astonishingly slow to update a breaking story.

Remember when parts of the northeast, including New York City, were hit by a massive electrical power failure one hot August afternoon in 2003? Television news was all over the story. But the next afternoon, CNN was still recycling video about the hardships people had faced 24 hours earlier.

On the second day of such a widespread power outage, a viewer might expect CNN and the others to tell us the latest news. Not so. They were still rehashing what happened the day before, showing and re-showing video of people walking home in a darkened city even though it was a day later, and the story offered completely new and different news angles.

And it has always been thus. As a young network news correspondent starting out at CBS News, I was counseled by Zeke Segal, a highly respected veteran assignment editor, to never get ahead of the story. He advised to always validate any major story by how it was approached or covered by the print news media. "We are and will always be the reaction side of journalism," he said referring to broadcast news.

Sadly that's still true today, despite amazing technological advances in newsgathering. The effect is compounded by the fact that contemporary television news is entertainment-driven. In many cities, "entertainment news" has the distinct flavor of Amateur Hour. Far too many of today's television anchors are nothing more than actors or readers with no journalistic training or credentials. Behind the scenes are news producers and interns with varying degrees of experience who are learning on the job. It is not surprising that the accuracy of reporting and the quality of writing on local television news are mediocre.

It is also not surprising then that TV news people feel safer about airing a story once they've seen it in print somewhere.

Even though impressive technological resources enable them to cover the news virtually anywhere on the planet, television news people do little original or enterprising reporting, focusing instead on recycling whatever appeared in the newspapers or wire services. Even breaking news, with its often-dramatic visuals, is generally covered in more depth by the print media and radio.

Now what about National Public Radio and newspapers? Whether at NPR headquarters in Washington or at their local stations around the country, a hallmark of National Public Radio is responsible, comprehensive, and compelling original journalistic reporting. Many diehard NPR listeners have forgotten the number of times they have been late to morning meetings at work because of sitting in their cars to hear the end of some story on the radio. They're called *parking-lot moments*, when you're arrived at your destination and remain glued to the car radio to hear the last of a riveting story.

National Public Radio is one of America's most influential news sources, and they have the audience numbers to prove it. NPR audience statistics will often eclipse major network television news programs.

Among those often spellbound by some story we hear on NPR are newspaper reporters, who are looking for good story ideas. If an

NPR story catches their interest, there's a good chance they will write about it. And then, of course, the TV news people will read about it in the paper, and the lemming effect by the news media will continue.

In strategic communications, a basic objective is to get your story before target audiences as responsibly and accurately as possible through the credible and influential conduit of the news media. You also want a reasonable degree of control over the story. And of course, you hope for good coverage. Consequently, television news is not the first place to take your story if you hope to have it air in an accurate manner.

You want to capitalize on the perception that when the media reports about you, you are seen as a leader. Consequently, when possible and appropriate in reaching out to the media, work first with public radio stations, commercial news/talk radio stations, newspapers, and wire services. There you generally will find today's best level of journalism, which will lead to more credibility and influence on important audiences.

PART TWO

ACHIEVE CLARITY IN A CLUTTERED WORLD

CHAPTER TWENTY

PERCEPTION IS THE HIGHEST FORM OF REALITY

Perception is the most powerful force in communications. We make decisions based on how we perceive something or someone. And no two perceptions are exactly alike. People can be poles apart in their perception of something, and both be "right," because their perceptions define their reality.

During our individual life journeys, we each have endless learning experiences and challenges that influence our perceptions.

You and I see a cloud. It reminds you of the Wyeth painting of a giant with a club; to me, it looks like rain coming. Two different perceptions, both correct up to a point and certainly our own truths.

The dictionary defines *perception* as "intuitive recognition of a truth." In fact, perception is far more complex, intangible and fragile than that.

When jockeying to capture audience awareness, too many companies look for a basic truth—or reality—in hopes it will set their organization apart from others: "we're the *leading* ..." or "the *largest* ..."

Unfortunately, this strategy lumps them into an enormous universe of other organizations saying the same thing. It's a boast that won't cut through competitive clutter. Journalists and savvy news consumers alike are alert to and suspicious of the overuse of superlatives, especially when the declarations are not backed up by a compelling track record. The overuse of self-aggrandizing adjectives used to be a popular style, especially among technology companies during the tech boom of the late nineties, yet, today, it often demotes potential for authentic credibility.

The conscious and subconscious factors that influence perception have been debated for centuries by academics and philosophers—and more recently, by the less skilled perspective of communications professionals. And still your perception of something tomorrow might be different than it is today and may have changed today from what it was yesterday. That's human nature and the nature of perceptions. We perceive events, people, companies, products, and things in different ways and we each are motivated by our individual perceptions.

Not surprisingly, understanding perception is critically important in practicing communications today. We want to, of course, strive for accuracy and clarity in what we tell the media, thus reducing chances for confusion and misperceptions. We may both be right when we see different things in the cloud; but in strategic communications, the perception that counts is that of the media.

Here's an example: If you have a policy that all comments to the media must be cleared by an attorney, then you could be building a perception with reporters of being defensive—that you've got something to hide.

The same is true if you read from a prepared statement in response to routine questions from reporters. Whether or not you read accurately, you are sending a signal of defensiveness. If your organization is already in hot water, you don't want to exacerbate the situation by acting evasive.

Here are six steps that I counsel companies, individuals, and organizations to take to enhance and manage a perception:

- *Get outside yourself.* Look at your image challenge from the perspective of an outsider, such as a client or customer or investor or the media. Understand how others see you.

- *Walk into the future.* Define how you want your organization to be described two or three years from now by people who are important to your company.

- *Challenge conventional thinking.* Just because something felt good a couple of years ago doesn't mean it will work in today's highly competitive arenas. It's OK—in fact, necessary—to discard bad habits in communications and try new approaches.

- *Avoid "committee speak."* Defining your organization by committee often results in too many words that say too little, too vaguely.

- *Steer away from overused 50-cent marketing words.* You know what they are: the dull adjectives pulled off the shelf when we can't think of anything else. Words like *unique, innovative,* and *leading provider* have been overworked to the point of becoming meaningless.

- *Be consistent.* Once you have decided what to say and how to say it, stick with that consistent approach in working with the news media. Consistency builds trust and helps overcome confusion that can adversely influence an otherwise good perception.

In striving for communications leadership, it doesn't matter whether you are the "largest" or the "best." If you are perceived as an organization that is communicating openly, candidly, and clearly, then you are sending positive signals to your audiences, including the news media. It helps you to be perceived as a winner.

CHAPTER TWENTY-ONE

NOTHING IS SECRET OR "NO COMMENT"

In today's world of e-mail, the Internet, and instant messaging, it's folly to think that anything is secret. Documents, notes from meetings, anything—regardless of the level of confidentiality—can be sent across town or around the world or show up on a blog in a flash with a single click of a mouse. It happens all the time.

What's more, there has been a proliferation of blogs devoted to finding out and revealing secrets about companies and organizations. MacRumors (MacRumors.com), for example, trades gossip, rumors and facts about Apple, the notoriously secretive computer company. Apple inspires considerable speculation among consumers, Wall Street and in the technology industry because of its penchant ... some call it, obsession ... for secrecy.

MacRumors has attracted such a large number of fans that it has been listed among the "25 most valuable blogs" on the Internet, and has become a money making venture for the site's founder, Dr. Arnold Kim. In fact, MacRumors is turning a nice profit through income from banner ads, commissions on product sales, and Google advertising, allowing Dr. Kim to move from his full-time job in medicine to earn a six-figure income as full-time blogger and work from home.

Success stories about popular and profitable blogs, like Mac Rumors, have spawned similar sites that focus on other organizations, because Apple is not the only company trying to keep secrets.

In strategic communications, the moment you sit down to write any document –whether a news release or strategic plan or e-mail—you must keep in mind that whatever you draft could become public, even inadvertently. Nothing is secret.

Throughout this book, I have stressed the importance of truthfulness and transparency in getting your story out and working with the news media. As I wrote earlier, communications with the news media mirrors behavior. An organization that dodges facts and manipulates issues will ultimately erode whatever credibility it may have.

What happened at the Washington, D.C., zoo is a classic example.

Under Dr. Lucy Spelman's watch as director of the National Zoo in Washington, nearly two dozen animals died, including some rare and endangered species. Some veterinary records were changed after the fact. In one case, a popular elephant died at an early age of tuberculosis for lack of an easily obtainable vaccination. In another case, two rare zebras died from hypothermia and malnutrition. It all came to light through a series of reports in the *Washington Post*.

How did the *Post* know? Somebody talked. A front-page story by Henri E. Cauvin had all the grisly details.

"In a confidential strategy paper produced by (PR agency) Hill & Knowlton, the zoo is urged to be open with the media but aggressive in containing any fallout from the deaths. The 23-page plan warns that continuing inquiries by the *Washington Post* could emerge as a story of national import, creating a crisis that would imperil the zoo's bid for full accreditation and threaten the job of Director Lucy H. Spelman.

"Lucy Spelman's credibility as a leader may appear to be diminished, with possible requests for her removal," Hill & Knowlton said in a list of potential scenarios that could follow more "negative news stories" on the zoo.

The result was that Spelman paid the PR firm $50,000 of the zoo's money to try to clean up her image, but it backfired. Her scheme became front-page news. It created a perception that good PR was more important than taking responsible and affirmative steps to ensure the safe welfare of zoo animals. Zoo employees were outraged by her behavior and confidential documents got into the hands of a reporter. The resulting series of stories portrayed Spelman as an inept zoo director and Hill & Knowlton as more concerned about her reputation than that of the zoo.

It didn't stop there. The arrogance of the zoo's leader resulted in a *Washington Post* editorial that began this way: "If only the animals could talk, we might learn more troubling truths about their care and feeding at the National Zoo. Incomplete or altered veterinary records have obscured instances of apparent neglect, misdiagnosis, and other serious mistakes in connection with the deaths of at least 23 animals...."

News is leaked to the media every day when unusual things happen. For example, in a rare peek behind the curtains of the Wal-Mart retail empire, the *New York Times* carried a front-page story about remarks made by the company's chief executive H. Lee Scott on a private, internal company Web site. A manager had asked him why the "largest company on the planet cannot offer some type of medical benefits." Scott, apparently annoyed, responded by accusing the manager of disloyalty and suggested he quit.

The exchange became public when copies of Scott's postings covering two years—two years!—were given to the *Times* by a group backed by unions and others pressing Wal-Mart to improve its employee wages and benefits.

Nothing—absolutely nothing—can be kept secret. The more egregious the sin, the more likely it will make it to the media. Remember the infamous Deep Throat of Nixon's Watergate, the Pentagon papers that the courageous Daniel Ellsberg released to the *New York Times* that exposed the cover-ups? That was more than 30 years ago, long before e-mail, blogs, the Internet, and a 24-hour news cycle. Secrecy is much harder today, if not nearly impossible, to pull off.

Apple, the computer company, takes secrets seriously. If an employee discusses a new product under development, for example, with anyone but a team member, the result is instant termination. It's all clearly spelled out for the company's employees who are required to sign confidentiality agreements.

At Apple, there is no leniency for employees who talk out of school. Tell a secret, and it's termination. Not surprisingly, Apple is noted for controlling the flow of news and announcements to the greatest benefit to the company.

Although you can't expect anything to be secret forever, you can maximize your chances of confidentiality and minimize your chances of damaging your reputation. Here are some tips on handling information before it goes public:

- *Label a draft as a draft.* When writing a document, such as a news release and media briefing document, type DRAFT at the top of the first page. Include draft version number, date, and your own initials. Then, if the document becomes public prematurely, your organization has a legitimate defense that the document was a draft, not a final statement.

- *Avoid e-mailing everyone.* It's a bad habit at many organizations to include extraneous people on e-mails. Limit e-mail daisy chains. Especially on issues of your organization's image and reputation, only share e-mails and documents between people who are relevant to the topic.

- *Have signed confidentiality statements.* Employees will often think twice before leaking sensitive material when they've signed a confidentiality statement that clearly spells out that termination may result from intentionally telling secrets.

Of course, the best safeguard in handling leaks is the time you invest in developing personal relationships with the reporters who cover your organization. You will develop credibility with the news media that will no doubt eclipse that of the informant.

There's nothing better in a potentially hostile media environment than to be on a first-name basis with key reporters. Having an established and trusted professional relationship with the news media can work to turn around wrong impressions, correct misinformation, help defuse a possibly unfavorable story, and provide a better and more accurate perspective for journalists.

If you are facing some tough issues that you will be asked about by the media and you want to shout, "No comment," you might as well hold up a big red sign that says, "Guilty!" The end result is about the same. It is simply irresponsible for a spokesperson to say, "no comment" because it will usually result in more damage.

Luladey Tadesse, a reporter at the Wilmington, Delaware, *News*

Journal, told me that "no comment" is really a comment. "It makes you look defensive," she said. She is so correct.

To a professional journalist, "no comment" can be a telltale sign of a bigger problem.

During 30 years as a journalist and strategic communications consultant, I can't tell you the number of times I've seen bad situations get worse because a spokesperson decided to say—usually in a curt tone of voice—"no comment" to the media rather than find a better response.

"No comment" immediately creates a feeling of fear and mistrust about an individual or organization, regardless of the circumstances.

It usually happens because some attorney mandates that the company say nothing but "no comment." It's irresponsible and shows disregard for an organization's brand image and reputation.

"The worst type of public relations person, usually found in-house at some organization, is the one who refuses to comment," said Jon Ashworth of *The Times* in London.

"No comment" suggests guilt, arrogance, and abruptness—all the emotional elements you want to avoid during a supercharged situation. It implies you have something to hide. Whatever the level of desperation, frustration, and aggravation when things go badly, those two words are never an option.

Here is an alternative approach to handling a potentially damaging situation for your organization:

First, when the phone rings and it's a reporter calling you, remember that there is no law that says you must talk with the reporter at that moment. If you feel unprepared or ambushed, buy some time to collect your thoughts and think of something to say. Explain to the reporter that you are more than happy to speak with him or her, but you are in the middle of something. Ask if he or she is on deadline and negotiate a reasonable time frame to return the call, such as a half hour to one hour.

Next—and this is essential—ask the reporter to give you an idea of what he or she wants to talk about. Never ask reporters what questions they are going to ask; just query the subject matter. Most reporters will work with you. Then get together with your public relations people and others to formulate a meaningful statement other than "no comment." Buying some time is an invaluable tool in strategic communications, because it allows you to get over being nervous about talking with a reporter, possibly over an adverse issue, and helps you to focus. Finally—and this is really important—contact the reporter as promised.

If your organization is facing an unfavorable situation that might draw media questions, it is essential to work in advance of any media contact and develop a response or statement, no matter how brief it might be. Think of it as a good opportunity to turn around a negative perception. A possible response could begin something like this: "While we are not prepared to make a formal statement at this time …" and then bridge one or two brief, important messages about the situation. In that way, you give the impression of being responsive, responsible, and accountable.

Lastly, remember that it's OK to be brief. In fact, the fewer words the better as long as they are not "no comment." The media will live with a response that's only a sentence or two because you are taking the time to at least say *something* during a difficult time. Consider a response that might elicit sympathy: "While this is a challenging time, we wanted to say …" and again bridge to a brief message.

A bridge is an interview tactic to control and redirect an interview back to the subject that you want to talk about, using the salient messages that you have developed and rehearsed in advance.

Whether you feel it or not, show genuine sincerity and a willingness to communicate. A positive attitude often will communicate as much as actual words. It may be your only constructive option.

If faced with a developing, possibly negative situation, why not say, "We want to be clear and accurate in anything we say. We are still gathering information that we will share with you when we have the whole picture."

In other words, there are many statements you can make to the news media other than "no comment." Those two words are not an option. View an adverse situation as an opportunity to briefly deliver positive messages that communicate responsiveness and concern.

CHAPTER TWENTY-TWO

OFF-THE-RECORD VERSUS BACKGROUND

I addressed "no comment" in the previous chapter. There also is no such thing as an "off-the-record" comment, particularly if you want to maintain some level of credibility. Unless you are employed by the White House or the National Security Agency, there's really no reason to talk off the record.

Based on my own experience as a journalist and listening to the comments of friends in the media, I advise clients to be wary of ever speaking off-the-record. The majority opinion within the media is that off-the-record comments can get too complicated and too fraught with hazards, particularly when all a reporter is seeking is a story. Strictly speaking, off-the-record means that nothing you have to say can be reported by a journalist. Nothing. So, in that context, there is no reason to be having the conversation. You would be wasting the reporter's time.

Nevertheless, I have seen occasions when less experienced newsmakers—often corporate executives—have suddenly proclaimed during an interview, "Now, off the record, let me say …" The only reason for the statement was, perhaps, to create a faux sense of gravitas or drama over an otherwise routine interview. But this disclaimer can be bewildering to a reporter, particularly if it's not in the logical flow of the interview subject or there is no purpose for it other than to create a false level of importance.

If you have something to share with the news media, there is seldom anything to be gained by attempting to speak off the record with a reporter. I know many journalists who will smartly refuse to allow interviewees to go off the record during an interview. When you talk off the record, integrity can be compromised, and enduring trust in a relationship with the media can be put to the test. The best advice is to avoid any off-the-record situation.

On the other hand, background briefings without attribution to a specific source have become commonplace, particularly in political and government circles. Background briefings are a valuable tool in communicating with the media today. We hear and read all the time statements that begin with phrases like "According to White House sources ..." or "Military commanders say ...."

Background briefings are helpful to the news media to provide perspective and depth of understanding about an issue, event, or story. A reliable source provides information, yet the name of the source really isn't important to the story.

A word of caution: Background briefings with the news media can be fraught with hazards. Anything you say in a background briefing can be reported, so there must be additional ground rules clearly agreed upon in advance. For example, in the background briefing, the name of your organization could be used unless you specify otherwise. Another risk is that you might forget to ask reporters not to use your name or job title.

If you have told a reporter that you will provide background without attribution, then whatever you say can be reported, but your name will not be used. If you forget to set the boundaries, then anything is fair game.

CHAPTER TWENTY-THREE

THE VALUE OF AN APOLOGY

I have never failed to be impressed by how a simple, honest apology can defuse the most volatile situation, often averting a communications crisis for a corporation or politician.

In another time, in the cowboy film *She Wore a Yellow Ribbon*, John Wayne growled "never apologize, and never explain." But that was then—more than 50 years ago in a macho western. This is now. Today apologies can do wonders.

Consider this example: "Gov. John Rowland changed his story Friday and acknowledged that friends—including some under suspicion in a federal corruption investigation—paid for work on his summer home," reported Susan Haigh of the Associated Press. "Rowland's admission, made public in a statement, came ten days after he insisted he alone had paid for improvements on the house at Bantam Lake."

Another politician confirms what we believe about most politicians: that they accept payoffs. Yet in this case, Rowland exacerbated his situation by lying, then changing his story, and announcing it in a written statement. A statement! Who's going to believe a written statement? Why not just come clean and stand up in front of the microphones and reporters with notebooks and say something that begins with, "I've made a terrible mistake. I apologize, and I'm going to do everything possible to make it right …."

Rowland was later found guilty and went to prison.

Equally astonishing is the absolute refusal by some organizations and titans of industry to ever admit to any mistakes, even when their hands are caught in the cookie jar. In fact, it seems that the larger the scope of misdoings and more egregious misconduct, the more likely that arrogance will prevent the perpetrators from even considering the value of an apology.

It must be something in the American ethos that a guy who makes an apology is some sort of "girlie man," to borrow Arnold Schwarzenegger's words. Attorneys advise clients to shun the actual word *apology* in favor of *regret*.

Did you ever hear an apology from Enron, Global Crossing, or Worldcom? Nope. The message we heard was one of blame and excuses, seemingly driven by greed and arrogance. We were left with the impression that many of those titans of business were just well-compensated crooks.

Another example: Hurricane Isabel cut a destructive swath up the east coast of the United States, leaving hundreds of thousands of people with no power for days. Several of the power companies were slow to restore service. It was disclosed in the media that they had cut back the number of repair crews needed to upgrade power lines in order to show a better bottom line to investors.

Rather than standing up in a news conference and saying simply, "We made a mistake. We apologize, and we are now working feverishly to restore electricity to your homes," the power-company executives attempted to defend their decisions. They did battle with the news media. They made the media their enemy rather than saying they screwed up. It was classic John Wayne behavior, circa 1950. Yet today such behavior comes off as incompetence and appears to emphasize greed over a clear focus on customer service. It wasn't smart, and the companies were broiled by the public, the media, the politicians and … the investors.

There are unfortunately far too many executives and attorneys who choose to duke it out (pun intended) with tough stances. The worse the situation, the greater the arrogance—and often the greater the media feast of one story after another. Denying responsibility or twisting facts, especially in the face of evidence to the contrary, will actually create a news story. Hey, just apologize, make amends, and move forward.

President George W. Bush managed to reduce damage to the reputation of his administration by accepting responsibility, albeit belatedly, for incompetence by the Federal Emergency Management Administration in responding to Hurricane Katrina in 2005. A week after the hurricane, people were still dying along the Gulf Coast, and the region was in chaos, because no aid had arrived from the federal government.

When it was apparent that the government had no plan and the administration was being scalded by everyone from the media to both Republicans and Democrats, Mr. Bush essentially said, "We were wrong, we made mistakes, but here's what we are doing now ..." and outlined a plan for assistance. Sadly, though, his apology was not subsequently linked to concrete actions and timely relief for those whose lives were devastated by the hurricane, giving rise to what some Bush administration observers called Bush's "smirk factor," a habit of making an apology or statement that is, in reality, neither sincere nor backed up by action.

Connecticut-based communications strategist Jane Genova counsels organizations on the value of creating goodwill through an apology. She said non-apologizers might be smart to explore using mea culpa as a power tool and she shared these examples from her work:

1. *Just observe.* When anyone makes a sincere apology, we listen. "I landed an assignment in the mega competitive hospitality industry by recognizing that even the most unhappy guest will be turned around by an authentic and detailed apology," she said.

2. *Give up on the "cult of the self."* Did the inward, self-focus theory ever work? It's questionable. In an interconnected, volatile global economy, who can go it alone? That's why the eastern philosophy of "no-self" is catching on rapidly. If we aren't defending the self, apology comes naturally.

3. *Decide if we want to be right, appear to be right, or be successful.* Surrendering on this one is the necessary inner paradigm shift that makes apology possible.

4. *Ignore the lawyers, initially.* We can apologize in ways that won't invite legal action or strengthen the case of the opposition. After we make a decision to do a mea culpa, then we should listen to the lawyers.

5. *Try out apologizing.* When we get the favorable attention of others out there, we know we're doing it right.

When talk show host Oprah Winfrey realized she had been duped by one of her chosen authors, James Frey, she accused him on live television of lying about the supposed facts in his book, *A Million Little Pieces*, and she apologized to her audience for originally endorsing the book. The high-profile celebrity knew the power of an apology; done right, it became disarming.

Unquestionably, a sincere apology has become an effective tool in practicing communications. Most everyone will give a break or second chance to someone who admits a mistake.

We are human. We do our best. We are not perfect. We make honest mistakes. In extremely difficult times, an apology can be an effective and proven method of controlling what the media says about you.

CHAPTER TWENTY-FOUR

THE CORPORATE COPY-CAT MENTALITY

Journalists who cover the high-technology industry have told me how often they note the lack of creativity by companies—from multinational giants to tiny startups—in describing new products and services. Earlier in this book, I compared the different approaches taken by Apple and Dell.

High-tech hopefuls, the companies that could really become future stars in the technology industry, often miss opportunities to capture meaningful earned media coverage that leads to all-important competitive differentiation.

This is a true story: The marketing communications staff at a software company was stumped, trying to figure out how to describe a new product that was being rushed to market after a competitor beat them to the punch. What could they say to capture the media's attention about their product? How could they create clever positioning? Words failed. But that wasn't all that failed.

Their boss got a brilliant idea: He instructed his staff to check the competitor's Web site and see how they had described their new product and then ... kinda, sorta ... plagiarize that description. Sound familiar? Unfortunately it's all too familiar in the technology industry. And it's a recipe for more failure. It's a strategy for landing yourself in second place ... or worse.

Everyone—the financial markets, investors, venture capitalists, and even ordinary people—likes technology because it's exciting and makes our lives easier and more manageable. When a company with substance comes along, technology can be a fun investment. And yet the high-technology world, with few exceptions, is too often a vast wasteland of blandness when it comes to distinctive and imaginative strategic communications.

No one is certain why, but technology has traditionally been wrapped up in talking about itself, using words that may sound impressive but mean little or nothing—"techno-babble," as one reporter called it.

Take a closer look at all the failed technological pioneers and, with few exceptions, you will find companies that pretty much used the same words and jargon to say the same things, regardless of their product or service. How many times have you heard phrases like "the world's leading innovative integrated systems solutions provider ..."

It's a lot like gas stations: When one gas station opens at an intersection, others follow, promoting themselves in the same way, saying the same thing. It's all copycat. Same with technology: When one tech company promotes itself with tired and overused 50-cent marketing words, others copy. The rest of us, seeing nothing authentic, get bored and lose interest.

In the practice of communications, when we get lazy and copy what a competitor is doing, we forfeit any chance to gain an edge and win. We lose any chance at competitive differentiation and leadership.

But despite all of this, technology not only holds the promise for America's success and security, it also has the opportunity to be an enduring darling of Wall Street. So here's an easy four-step checklist to help you authentically trumpet the true value of your enterprise—technology-related or not—and separate the leaders from the losers:

- *Think and talk outside of yourself.* Most of the time, the news media and your primary audiences prefer to hear about the value of what your organization does, rather than adjective-filled pronouncements about your company. Invest the time in some high-level strategic thinking to define how you want your company to be perceived and talked about in two or three years. That strategy will help to guide a positive, brand-building marketing communications approach today and into the future.

- *Make that strategic vision come alive.* Develop an original, practical, and working strategic plan that uses clever tactics to gain attention to credibly and realistically achieve what's called *competitive positioning.* Remember, it doesn't really matter whether you are the "largest" or "best" organization. If you are viewed as a leader, you've won.

- *Stand in the shoes of your audiences.* Learn how to communicate the benefit of your product or service to the person who ultimately makes the decision and has the authority to buy.

- *Talk in sound bites, not elevator speeches.* A sound bite communicates your message or describes your endeavor, precisely, in one breath—about 16 seconds—while using words that are understandable, credible, exciting, and memorable. An *elevator speech,* although popular, takes too long—particularly if you are headed for the 44th floor. Reporters, distracted by others who can say it concisely, will lose interest.

- *Avoid junk words—jargon, acronyms, buzzwords, and trendy clichés.* Few phrases lead to more communication confusion and misunderstandings than the prefabricated and empty clichés of business and management consultants, such as *value proposition, actionable, learning partners, ramp-up, empowering, maximizing, critical path,* and *visioning.* It's a long list of ambiguous "junk" words that probably originated in some business school years ago. Yet, in today's preference for transparency and plain language, junk words are to be avoided. They can impede clear communication.

When used properly, these principles of effective communications work not just for technology companies, but for any organization. Strategic communications requires clear and precise differentiation so that the media and audiences know you from your competitor.

The challenge is to overcome a common thread among most

companies: the inability to incisively and concisely describe their individual value and what's genuinely special about what they deliver to their audiences—their customers. Too often the company stalls in its own words and business-school jargon.

When technology and other industry sectors occasionally run out of gas—and they can—it's your job to fill up their tanks with high-octane creativity. Throw in a wash and wax, and get back out on the racetrack using timely and compelling communications with journalists that make positive news for your organization.

Perhaps one of the most common "sins" of leaders and communications people is never actually identifying how to bridge the gap between what is *newsworthy* for the media and the promotional message they push on behalf of a client or employer.

Consequently, too many, if not most, media campaigns are centered around—maybe it's more accurate to say hidden behind—a systematic flood of news releases and expensive media materials that are sent out carpet-bomb style to the media, most often to the wrong people.

Many organizations have been sending out press releases for so long that it has become part of the corporate culture, regardless of whether it is effective. Public relations people are aware of old habits but rarely suggest more contemporary techniques for generating earned media coverage because to help a client distribute a press release is simple work for a junior staffer. It is easy billable time.

It happens hundreds of times each day: An organization issues a news release via a paid news release wire service, such as PR Newswire or BusinessWire, or through a service that bulk e-mails thousands of news contacts. Those e-mails are often caught in spam filters and are never seen. Somehow, there is a feeling that if the news industry is smothered by a release, someone might pay attention. On the contrary, such mass distribution is an unproductive way of getting the attention of today's news media—and about as effective as dropping thousands of copies of the release from an airplane except that the latter might actually get some news coverage ... albeit not so positive, I suspect.

Out of fairness, mass distribution of financial news announcements—for example earnings reports and news of market and shareholder interest—provide an efficient way to meet disclosure requirements.

If you hope that a news release will somehow become a meaningful news story—whether in a newspaper, blog, TV newscast, or anywhere else—I must respectfully inform you that you are mistaken. If you pay a press release distribution service to send your release to the news universe, you are taking the wrong approach and wasting money.

Journalists are paid to find fresh new stories that competitors don't have. Mass distribution means everyone has the same information. *USA Today* is typical of today's media—if you send them a news release that you have sent to everyone else or pitch a story that you have pitched to other news organizations, they will not touch it regardless of how great it might sound. Why should they pay any attention to your news release that you have shared with the world?

Nonetheless, the paid news-distribution services are also clogged with other poorly focused and irrelevant news releases that journalists tend to ignore many, if not most, of the releases because they just do not have the time to sort through all of them.

If there is one common trait among many people who are charged with working with the media, it is a reluctance to actually interface personally with the news media in any way, such as through a phone call. Odd as it might seem, too many public relations people hide behind news releases, media lists, mailings, bulk e-mails, and faxes. They avoid actually picking up the phone to speak with a journalist to develop a working relationship.

Organizations spend fortunes on so-called news-distribution services to get their news releases and media materials in front of as many journalists as possible, seemingly to help them avoid having to go to the trouble of picking up a phone and making a personal pitch to a reporter.

It's fairly common to hear PR agency executives tell their clients that an "exclusive" news service was used to get their release before several thousand reporters, as if to suggest that the PR people have somehow managed to stop the presses and get the attention of hordes of reporters who read their client's news announcement. Such claims can only be labeled as "murky truth." While a news distribution service might have the capability to send a news release to thousands of journalists via e-mail, there's no guarantee that anyone will actually really read it or even consider doing a story, much less the release ever resulting in a story.

Today an increasing number of savvy executives and strategic communications professionals are turning to newer and alternative approaches to produce meaningful results. These new approaches do not require sending out hundreds of news releases. The process begins by crafting a legitimate news story, then focusing on only that handful of journalists who cover an organization. The technique is to build trusted relationships with journalists, provide incisive information, and set the stage to work with those journalists to develop a relevant and timely news story. That's the way to maximize control of your story and improve the chance it will come out the way you hope.

"Don't overwhelm the assignment desk and producers with too much information," counsels C-SPAN's Steve Scully. "With all the paperwork we deal with everyday, less is better. Accurate and *timely* is required."

The traditional wisdom among PR people that "more is better" is both ineffective in contemporary strategic communications and often annoying to journalists. Working effectively with the media today mandates approaching the right journalist with the right story angle at the right time. It requires making a personal contact rather than hiding behind paper.

A general manager of a local National Public Radio station tells friends she has built a terrific library at home with all the books sent to her over the years by book publicists who never made a phone call to figure out who to send a book to in order to schedule an on-air interview with the author. She got on the publicity mailing list and received a ton of books. By the way, the general manager or station manager is never the right person to contact.

Some book publicists may still take that passive approach but book promotion is one area that is quickly embracing the use of blogs and RSS content management Web sites to drive awareness for new books. It is partly because using such technology delivers faster search engine optimization and online visibility. I see it first-hand as Publisher and Co-Founder of BoomerCafé.com, the popular online magazine for baby boomers with active lifestyles. Each day, we are pitched by book publicists who have read our story submission guidelines and are aggressive to provide all the elements we need for a story, including links to author blogs. What they are doing not only is selling books but delivering revenue to their companies.

Typical news media materials, on the other hand, begin with a form-type generic cover letter that explains the critical importance of the news from the sender's perspective. The letters generally have an urgent stop-the-presses tone about them and suggest that this news is the greatest announcement since Al Gore supposedly invented the Internet. More often than not, the cover letter fails to suggest how this so-called news might actually be made into a news story. Sadly for the hopeful writer, these news materials are pushed aside by items that carry a more genuine tone or are more professionally presented.

Most journalists prefer a specific, personalized story pitch rather than a news release. So many news people have said they need "an idea that is news-driven" rather than a typical fluffy news release.

"Give me numbers, think of other possible sources, and even give sources who might be on the other side. That is really helpful. What is the controversial point, who might we want to talk to on the other side?" said a wire-service reporter.

Pat Piper produced "The Larry King Show" for more than a decade on Mutual Radio and today collaborates with King on a variety of books. He thinks most PR people oversell to the media and compulsively send too much "stuff."

"Here's a newsflash," Piper said. "The world may revolve around your client but the world I deal with doesn't usually include your client or cause. I always have a trash can when I open the mail. I always have a delete button when I read an e-mail attachment."

Denver-based newspaper columnist and HDNet news correspondent Greg Dobbs gives this useful advice: "Ask yourself what the media wants and needs. The answer won't necessarily be the message you want to communicate, but if you don't get them 'in the door,' the strongest message on earth will have no impact.

"How do you figure out what the media wants and needs? Simple: pretend you are a reporter, and your only stake in the matter is in getting a good story, not in getting your message out. In other words, put yourself in the reporter's shoes and offer what he or she is looking for. In short, get their attention, then work on carving that message."

Communicating to today's media is not blitzing everyone in the newsroom with the same news release or media kit. It all comes down to establishing a trusted relationship—making a phone call to the news organization, identifying the right reporter, and presenting an interesting, timely and relevant story in the brief and incisive manner that reporters prefer.

Chapter Twenty-Five

A Time to Question Bad Habits

Some corporations and organizations are following the misguided trend—call it a bad habit—of using news releases and other materials under the guise of working with the news media but that actually manipulate credibility. It's about *safe-harbor* statements, which are tantamount to saying, "nothing you are about to read is true," and *about* statements, which are blatant self-promotion. Both adversely impact credibility in dealing with the news media.

The idea of including in news releases a piece of legal language called a safe-harbor statement gained popularity in the mid-1990s with high technology companies. Their attorneys believed the companies needed protection from themselves and from many of the often-outlandish claims they made in news releases and other promotional materials. In other words, their own attorneys questioned whether the bravado of tech companies was truthful.

So the attorneys came up with standard safe-harbor language, or boilerplate, to be included at the end of every news release, that they hoped would legally protect a company from being accused of outright lying. Here's an example of a safe-harbor statement from a technology company:

> This press release may include statements that may constitute "forward-looking statements," including its estimates of future business prospects or financial

results and statements containing the words "believe," "estimate," "project," "expect," or similar expressions. Forward-looking statements inherently involve risks and uncertainties that could cause actual results of this company and its subsidiaries (collectively, the "Company") to differ materially from the forward-looking statements. Factors that could contribute to such differences include: the ability of the Company to implement and achieve widespread customer acceptance of its Report Services software on a timely basis; the Company's ability to recognize deferred revenue through delivery of products or satisfactory performance of services; continued acceptance of the Company's products in the marketplace; the timing of significant orders; delays in the Company's ability to develop or ship new products; market acceptance of new products; competitive factors; general economic conditions; currency fluctuations; and other risks detailed in theCompany's registration statements and periodic reports filed with the Securities and Exchange Commission. By making these forward-looking statements, the Company undertakes no obligation to update these statements for revisions or changes after the date of this release.

In 186 words or about 20 percent of the total content of the news release, the company warns, "Reader, beware!" It's a classic cover-your-butt approach, and it is often a deal-breaking if you are attempting to establish any level of credibility with the media. A journalist takes one look and understandably wonders whether anything in the news release is true.

Ask a reporter what they think of about statements, as I have, and they will tell you that it's usually common information easily found with a couple of clicks on the organization's Web site.

In fact, what I have heard consistently from journalists is that they prefer to find background about an organization from online newsrooms or Google searches, not in news releases. All the fluffy, self-serving promotion included in news releases is ignored for what it is—useless information not relevant to a story.

By the way, the simpler an online newsroom is to navigate and the more specific contact and timely information you offer to reporters in one location, the easier it is for reporters to write about your organization. Dynamic content management platforms and RSS online technology used on an organization's online news info site will help reporters track updates with automatic newsreaders. That ultimately can translate into increased coverage.

There is, however, a significant gap between what journalists expect to find on corporate Web sites and what PR practitioners actually provide.

Today's savvy managers and strategic communications professionals can make everything easily available online, including media kits, corporate backgrounders, fact sheets about services or products, photos and visuals, case studies, and even bylined feature stories. Yet some old and very boring corporate habits are hard to break.

One major department store chain, for example, includes a 225-word boilerplate about the corporation at the end of every news release even though the company, founded more than 100 years ago, is a global brand. The company's about statement has no relevance to any news announcement and is something that could easily included at an online newsroom.

So, I telephoned the company's corporate communications department to learn why the company feels the need for the boilerplate, and got this explanation:

"It's just something standard we do. All our competitors do, so we must too," I was told.

But is it relevant for every news release, I asked?

"No, I guess not but we've just gotten into the habit of adding it to all releases," was the response.

Sometimes an organization's communications team needs to question bad habits and copycat styles.

Journalists suggest that companies should just focus on "news" in a news release and not use the forum to advertise and promote.

This seems logical, but at many organizations, corporate rationale, with a compulsive eye on sales and promotion, takes a different view.

The position seems to be "if our attorneys think we're going to the edge of believability anyway, we might as well go all the way and use news releases for sales purposes."

In companies where public relations is under the control of the marketing department, the trend of marrying about and safe-harbor statements has gotten completely out of control. There is one software company, for example, that includes a voluminous 200-word boilerplate about statement at the end of its news releases that is full of puffy adjectives trumpeting the company's glory and its products. The length of the company's about promotion rivals the length of the actual news content. Yet, this tech company is by no means alone.

The about boilerplate is a trend that has become commonplace at too many organizations, who apparently think news releases are just another type of sales collateral material.

Among journalists, standard boilerplate potentially creates the impression that a company is not making the effort to develop anything truly newsworthy; they are just embedding a commercial message in a news release for self-promotion.

What organizations don't seem to realize is that news releases are targeted for the news media, not potential customers. News releases are not sales brochures or advertisements or billboards. News releases are intended to announce legitimate *news*.

After all, what's the purpose of the news release—to communicate real news or distribute promotional fluff? If your answer is the latter, consider protecting your organization's credibility by passing the assignment off to the marketing department and advise them to buy an ad.

Veteran C-SPAN television producer Scott Scully wants news releases that are credible and concise. "Send *accurate* information to the assignment desk," he said. "This means the correct date and time … contact person and *relevant* information."

News releases can be most effective when used to announce timely and relevant information that affects an organization's audiences. In today's highly competitive world, where the image of an organization rests on convincing and accurate words, too much is at stake to mess with credibility by bastardizing a news release for self-promotional agendas.

It all comes back to the traditional intent of a news release, that bridge for communicating with the media. You must understand, above all, that a release is all about providing accurate news to help journalists develop a story.

If the news release content is accurate, truthful, and timely, there is no journalistic or legal reason for a safe-harbor statement. Just tell the news.

And about the imagined need for that about boilerplate in a news release, let's get real. The unique value and competitive positioning of any company, organization, issue, or cause on the planet can be described in fewer than a dozen quotable and memorable words, easily embedded as a phrase within the actual news release copy. If it drones on much longer, it becomes a speech or a full-blown advertorial.

Over and over, journalists say that the best form of media relations is relationship-based, when a person responsible for working with the media simply stays in touch with a circle of reporters who are interested in his or her organization. As stated earlier in this book, news releases are no substitute for getting to know the right journalists.

News releases are to announce news, not to be used as advertising flyers. Always tell the truth and you won't need to hide behind an attorney or a safe harbor that might turn out to be too shallow.

CHAPTER TWENTY-SIX

CONTENTIOUS WORDS ARE THOUGHT-STOPPERS

I have always loved to read Mark Twain. About the craft of writing, he told a friend, "I notice that you use plain, simple language, short words, and brief sentences. That is the way to write English—it is the modern way and the best way. Stick to it; don't let fluff and flowers and verbosity creep in. When you catch an adjective, kill it."

It has long been important to many companies and organizations to claim—especially when describing themselves in news releases, interviews, and marketing materials—that they are "the largest" or "the best" or "the leading" or whatever.

Companies often spend enormous amounts of time guessing the best words to use. They exhaust themselves with such prattling, attempting to make it stick and convince us that they are the greatest outfits on the planet and can find solutions that others cannot.

Such contentious claims and words seldom fly. A boast to be the best at anything often causes a listener or reader to stop in their tracks and question whether it's true or not. While stopped to think about a boast, the audience seldom will hear anything further. Organizations need to remember Twain's advice to kill the adjectives.

One of today's most effective trends in communications is the use of plain language, free of acronyms, claims that cannot be proved, and boastful adjectives.

Remember all the dot-com and technology companies of the late 1990s? With negligible track records or earnings, they all claimed to be "the most advanced" or "the leading integrated service provider." And where are they now? Their claims were not believable. Many were also not true. Most are now history.

Yet, we continue to hear it even today, such as "the leading systems integrator and information technology company, bringing seamless solutions …" Blah, blah, blah. As an audience, we tend to tune out or look for alternatives.

If I were to tell you that I am "the smartest man on earth," your ability to listen to and believe what I was saying would likely stop at that point. I might continue talking and provide numerous reasons to support my claim, but chances are you would still be questioning the word "smartest." You wouldn't be listening to me but rather compiling a list in your mind of the many other people far smarter than me. My claim would lack credibility and everything else I might attempt to say would be dismissed.

When we hear boastful words, it is a natural impulse to stop where we are and immediately question their validity.

Boastful words are contentious and the use of contentious words in communications impedes the effectiveness of how you reach an audiences. On the other hand, plain language, free of adjectives, captures favorable attention; audiences listen.

The best of all worlds is when a respected third-party says nice things about you, using plain language. That is something that gets attention. People listen and are likely to share what they have just heard with a friend or colleague.

A company claims to be outstanding, however, and we quietly think to ourselves, "Well, I can think of a dozen other companies that are better," ignoring whatever else the company tries to say.

When someone or an organization brags in the media, they are not only being contentious and risking the chance the media might ignore them as a result; they are also gambling with their credibility. One single contentious word or phrase can stop effective communication. It's like calling the blind with a three and a five, off suit, in a poker game of Texas Hold 'Em. You've really got nothing … but talk.

With full knowledge that I am entering possibly hostile waters here, I will say that, as a broad and sweeping generalization, attorneys seldom make for good spokespeople when left unchecked or without the counsel of a seasoned communicator. I've seen attorneys make powerful presentations in court only to walk outside to a battery of microphones and cameras and become incapable of putting together a lucid, easy to understand summary of the case—in words that a lay audience might understand. Attorneys often speak a language that is only comfortable to them—legalese—and they leave audiences either confused or in the dark.

I should add quickly that I have worked with some outstanding attorneys who enthusiastically welcomed interview technique coaching and today do an admirable job whenever in front of a microphone, camera, or gaggle of reporters.

However, many continue to use legalese. I have heard some people say that the issue is ego. I do not agree, completely. The problem, I believe, is that many attorneys lack thorough understanding and respect for the power of the media as a communications medium and, consequently, have never taken the time to learn how to speak with the media. As a result, they are left at a disadvantage and not able to intellectually shift gears from legal speak to plain language that people outside a courtroom can understand. It is a translation challenge. Many attorneys also don't comprehend the communications value of a sound bite; they generally don't care and wouldn't know how to compose one if their lives depended on it.

Whether speaking with broadcast reporters, print journalists, or bloggers, what the media seeks is an interesting summary in plain language. They want you to incisively sum up an issue by getting to the point, first.

A sound bite gets right to the point of what you have to say, then is supported by a brief summary. From my experience as a journalist and communicator, I would define a sound bite as: describing your endeavor, precisely and in a captivating way, in one breath—about 16 seconds—while using words that are understandable, credible, interesting, and memorable.

The media cherishes sound bites. Reporters agree that a great sound bite will bring a story to life. Today's politicians, it seems, prefer to talk in nothing but sound bites, because they want to make news.

Sound bites are the communications technique of getting to the bottom line of what you have to say; they are unquestionably one of the best ways to get into print and on television and radio newscasts. *Sound bites get to the heart of the story.* The journalist can then always ask more questions and fill in all the details if they choose.

By contrast, many attorneys speak primarily legalese, a vague-sounding, verbose, ambiguous, and somewhat evasive language that not a lot of us, including the news media, understand. Attorneys presumably comprehend what they are saying and other attorneys may, too. Legalese comes from their training. But most of us don't understand legalese; it is not everyday plain language.

Unquestionably, some attorneys remain distrustful of the media. I can only say, from my experience, that they have not invested the time to understand how to become effective communicators or to fully comprehend the massive power of today's media to reach audiences. In some ways, I suppose, they are not fully representing the welfare of their clients because of their lack of knowledge of the media's role in communications today.

The mixture of legalese with arrogance, which too often is the signature of attorneys, is a destructive cocktail in media relations. Yet many times we've seen an attorney speaking in what seems like a pompous manner to "set the record straight" on behalf of a client or organization. I don't know about you, but I sometimes find myself wanting to root for the other guy.

There are, of course, exceptions. Reporters enjoy interviewing attorneys who can demonstrate skill at interpreting often-complicated legal opinions and theory into words that are clear and concise. Washington, D.C., attorney Thomas Wilner is one of the best. Wilner represented Kuwaiti men held at Guantánamo Bay by the United States without access to due process rights, a controversial case that reached the United States Supreme Court.

In discussing that case on the PBS *NewsHour*, this is how Wilner responded to a reporter's question about the meaning of habeas corpus:

> "Habeas corpus was really a fundamental right developed under the common law. It really was to enforce the rights granted by the Magna Carta. The Magna Carta said that no person shall be deprived of his liberty without

jury by his peers and accordance with the law of the land and habeas corpus was developed to enforce that. Really what it does, it requires judicial review, independent review of the facts and circumstances to see whether there's a reason to hold somebody."

In this interview, Wilner translated possibly confusing legal language and terminology clearly into words that everyone can comprehend.

Attorneys like Wilner provide the best representation for their clients, especially at times when client issues are of interest to the media. They understand the media communication process. They can give essential guidance and suggestions on wording and opinions about legal issues to their clients and when briefing the media. They can help to identify potential minefields and problems well in advance.

The language of law needs to be translated into words, phrases, and thoughts that more effectively communicate with broad audiences we are seeking to reach, inform, and motivate, including the media.

In my work, both as a journalist and in public relations, I've found only a handful of attorneys who are skilled at delivering concise messages to the media in layman's terms. Rather than working with communicators to find interesting ways to generate coverage, many attorneys actually impede the image and media outreach efforts of their clients or companies by coming up with laundry lists of improbable scenarios and finding reasons why doing anything would be a bad idea.

Lawyers are too prone to thinking defensively and trying to persuade an organization into "no comment" mode, even when there's nothing to fear in communicating with the news media. As stated in a previous chapter, "no comment" only builds fear and mistrust about an organization. In strategic communications, it's not an option.

Lawyers have a place in the strategic communications process, and we are starting to see change on the horizon as more attorneys recognize the power and value of knowing how their words can make news.

People who work in strategic communications should establish working relationships with attorneys. Seek their counsel, consider the opportunities, and think about what's best for your organization and your audiences and your stakeholders. And if you are stuck with an attorney as a spokesperson, get them some media training *first*.

When dealing with the news media, we need to communicate as clearly and accurately as possible. We need to get to the point, using plain language. Legal speak is seldom convincing when working with the media, and all too often can cause confusion by its complex language and jargon.

PART THREE

DEVELOP A DISTINCTIVE
VOICE OF LEADERSHIP

CHAPTER TWENTY-SEVEN

THE PILLARS OF SAVVY COMMUNICATIONS LEADERSHIP

The process of developing an organization's strategic communications cannot be delegated to staff members who may not be aware of the whole picture. Today's executive leader needs to be involved, at least in defining the vision that he or she wants to communicate, and the primary positioning messages to precisely differentiate the organization from competitors.

Strategic communications planning is a process that need not be difficult or time-consuming.

Think of the pillars of effective strategic communications as three legs on a stool that allow you to stand above the crowd and be seen. Take away one or two legs, and you'll fall off. Add too many legs, and the stool becomes awkward and unmanageable. Here are the three pillars:

Pillar One: The Strategic Communications Plan. A plan gives focus to your purpose and your objectives. Why would any organization ever consider launching an outreach program, issuing a news release, or making any public statement without some sort of plan that provides purpose, relevance, and context?

Without a plan, public statements or promotional announcements usually lack focus and actually work against an organization's overall marketing and business objectives. You could be compromising your company's reputation. So why would you say anything in public without a plan? I cannot think of any reason except for carelessness or ambivalence about your organization's image. Nonetheless, many companies crank out news release after news release, often without rhyme or reason.

Effective strategic communications begins with a carefully thought-out plan to competitively position an organization. The plan embraces the overall corporate vision and objectives and gives focus, purpose, and reason to a communications effort. It does not begin with tactics or with copying tactics that you've seen other people use to boost visibility in the media. It begins with asking yourself candid and tough questions that will help you really put your fingers on the distinct pulse of your organization and identify precisely the right ways and the best words to enhance your image before key audiences. Some of those questions are:

- What's so special about your organization that makes it stand out from anyone else, and who cares beyond the company parking lot?

- What are the things about your company that appeal most to the people who really matter outside and who rely on your organization, such as customers and stakeholders?

- How do you want your company talked about, in clear, jargon-free words? In other words, how do you think your best customer might describe why you were chosen over a competitor?

- What is genuinely newsworthy about your organization and what it does or produces?

Think of a strategic communications plan as a beacon that will guide your important messages and vision about your organization to audiences and stakeholders. A strategic communications plan mirrors the objectives of a company's business plan and works to bring the strategic business plan to life more efficiently and more compellingly than any other method.

The plan's components are straightforward:

- *Situation overview*: a few paragraphs to summarize the lay of the land, competitive environment, challenges and obstacles, and advantages and opportunities. This is your opportunity to say, "Here's what we're going to do and how we're going to make it happen."

- *Audiences*: a list of all audiences that you intend to reach through your media initiative—internal and external, public and highly specialized. I've always observed a natural tendency to create a list that's too long yet often omits the news media. Sometimes we even list an audience group that's no longer relevant to our business. Here's your chance to fine-tune that list and reduce it to the essentials.

- *Positioning message*: an introductory sentence or two that distinctly and clearly differentiates you from your competitors and will work to capture the attention of your key audiences. (For more on positioning messages, see the next chapter.)

- *Objectives*: preferably three and certainly no more than four goals that reflect and complement the aim of your organization's business plan. Begin each objective with an active word, such as *boost* or *enhance* or *create*. You can also use the old style of beginning each objective with the word *to*.

- *Strategies*: a specific strategy for achieving each objective. This is where you describe in detail how you intend to achieve the objectives—in other words, how you plan to get from here to there. Remember that you cannot list an objective without a strategy for making it happen.

- *Tactics*: unique and distinctive action points that will bring your strategies to life in order to achieve the objectives.

- *Measurement*: a mechanism to demonstrate tangible results. Elements can include an upward trend in news stories, increased Web site traffic, and more unsolicited contact from journalists. Create a *measurement matrix*, a chart that tracks each component and clearly shows achievements.

- *Timeline:* how will the plan be executed in a timely fashion, and when can you expect to start seeing results.

Be mindful of not allowing tactics to drive the planning process. *Tactics are the fun side of planning, while objectives and strategies require more thought.* Consequently, people all too often jump to tactics that may or may not be relevant to the plan. That could lead to wasted time, wrong strategic directions, and costly mistakes.

Let me digress for a moment to talk about objectives, strategies, and tactics and to provide an example.

An objective might be driving to the beach for the weekend.

A strategy is how you are going to make it happen, such as planning the shortest trip at the best time to avoid traffic. There is always just one strategy to achieve each objective.

Tactics are the actions, items, or steps needed to bring a strategy to life and for accomplishing an end, such as, in this example, finding the car keys, bringing a roadmap, putting your suitcase in the trunk, and finding a roadmap.

During the process of developing a plan, the right tactics will naturally reveal themselves. Chances are you can even identify clever new tactics that will become distinctive to your organization. So even if someone else currently has an advantage over you in the area of media relations, it's realistic to expect to gain the upper hand, because many people don't bother to develop a smart plan. I've found that most people think only about tactics, such as a news release, and hope that will solve everything. Before you think about tactics, think big. Develop a strategy.

Once you've launched that process, you will begin to see your company through a new set of eyes, with twenty-twenty vision, focused on the essence of what's important. You will no longer find it relevant to think of your organization in terms of competitors but rather as a unique organization of talented people who are part of something big.

Pillar Two: Be Original. While it always helps to know your competition, ignore what they are saying and how they are saying it. Although a competitor may do something cool, it may not be either smart or effective. If there's a news story about them, and you are not mentioned, forget it. As with the city bus, another opportunity will soon come along before you know it. If you copy or react to the featured organization, you have, by default, put yourself in second place, making yourself a "wannabe" in the media's eyes. The news media and the public don't like wannabes.

Ignore how the competition talks to the media. Chart new territory. Be original and imaginative, because you are smarter and savvier than they are.

There's too much competitive clutter out there in the marketplace these days. You cannot afford to be ordinary. Throw out conventional wisdom and traditional approaches to the techniques for working with the media. I've often said that conventional wisdom is a code phrase for dull and predictable.

Challenge the claims and promises of your public relations agency, if you have one. Forget news releases and expensive media kits. Don't fall into the trap of feeling compelled to announce every little event that happens at your place. Your organization has special things to say, so why say them in a predictable and boring fashion?

An essential part of being original is to use clever visuals. If you want to quickly leapfrog your brand out ahead of your competition, think about three things: visuals, visuals, visuals. Nothing captures the media's attention faster than great pictures. When it comes to what makes it on the air, a TV news producer most often will go with a second-class story that has great visuals over a better story without visuals. That's just the way journalism works, and it's not going to change. Television news is driven completely by visuals over content.

These days, print journalism is more focused on appealing visuals as well. *USA Today* created a whole new way of using color, graphics, and pictures when it debuted in the early 1980s, and most other newspapers and magazines have followed suit and improved on the trend. The fastest way into the business section of a major daily newspaper is with a story that has a compelling photo. Most business editors could not care less about the introduction of a new automobile, but when the car maker's chief executive officer and his top designer are seated on the front of the car in a photo, and a crisply written story about the smart teaming of the two executives is provided with it, editors pay attention.

Pillar Three: Tell the Truth. Regardless of the situation and circumstances, accuracy, transparency, and candor in dealing with the media is always the best route.

Ever since the technology bubble burst in the early part of this decade, pundits have debated the possible reasons why it happened. Certainly there were numerous financial and market forces at work, not the least of which was the massive overvaluation of many technology stock offerings—valuations that were based on nothing more than a promise and a prayer. But the most fundamental reason, in my opinion, was the untruthful way in which so many tech companies were promoted to the news media.

In the rock 'n' roll environment of the high-flying late 1990s, when everything about technology companies—literally everything from balance sheets and business plans to marketing claims and stock performance—was overstated or nonexistent, communications with the media was also hyped. Many CEOs made grandiose claims based on concocted and sometimes downright false information, and few people raised questions. The climate was right. Business reporters, bored of covering the traditional stories, were all of a sudden being hustled by exciting new companies and ideas. They took the bait and bought all the hype. The stories seemed too good not to believe. Everyone—from venture capitalists to analysts to the markets—seemed to validate the high-flying news. Of course, as it turned out, the venture capitalists and analysts and markets were all making tons of money directly from the tech companies.

But in the end, contempt for the truth spelled downfall. Ultimately the truth will come out. From the perspective of journalists I have spoken with, failed technology and other companies have no one to blame but themselves for their demise. Greed eclipsed truth and accuracy. And we have seen the fallout: markets and investors skittish of any tech venture, even at the expense of the handful of companies out there who might be making money with a unique product or service. The once ever-so-smug leaders of tech during that era nearly killed an entire industry by not telling the truth.

Today, we are living in a completely different era. In today's world of communicating through the media—when what you say can be heard around the world in a split second—imaginative ideas, transparency, and the truth win out over thread-worn conventional wisdom, such as manipulation, parsing words, and hype, every day of the week.

Today's most highly visible and respected business leaders have invested the time to develop a plan for competitive brand leadership. They have dared to step outside the box of what everyone else is doing and saying in order to capture awareness with imaginative ideas and approaches. Most of all, they are earning our trust and respect by being open and transparent.

CHAPTER TWENTY-EIGHT

MISSION STATEMENTS VERSUS POSITIONING MESSAGES

If there is one issue that separates today's savvy leader from wannabes, it is recognizing the meaningless value of mission statements when what an organization really desires is better brand awareness.

Mission statements. "A bunch of guys take off their ties and coats, go into a motel room for three days, and put a bunch of words on a piece of paper—and then go back to business as usual."

Nothing I have researched has ever more accurately described the usually meaningless exercise of an organization attempting to come up with a mission statement than this quote that has been attributed to John Rock, an executive for more than three decades at the now-defunct Oldsmobile Division of General Motors.

My take of mission statements, based on years of corporate consulting, is that most are trivial and fail to help lead an organization, improve a brand, or increase competitive success.

If you really read them closely, mission statements don't make a lot of sense.

They are frequently a pastiche of buzzwords designed to sound lofty, reassuring, authoritative, and, well, boring. The end result too often is a "Who cares?" effect.

Pamela Goett, who worked for the Journal of Business Strategy, dug into the origins of mission statements and has written this reality check:

"A handful of years ago, some guru opined that mission statements were absolutely critical to a company's success. So a lot of firms pack their most senior people off to expensive retreats to prepare this vital document. And the executives took the task very, very seriously (which is why so many mission statements sound so stuffy). The hoopla over mission statements and vision has a lot in common with the cheers for the emperor's new clothes. It's applause for delusions, for quick fixes for something that needs more thought and planning than can be expressed in a calligraphic paragraph."

It has been said that organizations invest otherwise productive time to develop mission statements when they don't know who they are or why they are special.

Jack Trout, a management strategist who really knows what he is doing, dissects the standard five phase process of creating a mission statement this way. His comments are in italics:

Phase 1: Envision the future: *It can't be done.*
Phase 2: Form a mission task force: *Waste of time of expensive people.*
Phase 3: Develop a draft statement: *Many hands make things mushy.*
Phase 4: Communicate the final statement: *Hang it on the wall for people to ignore.*
Phase 5: Operationalize the statement: *Turn the company into mush.*

Everybody, however, seems to need a mission statement these days, and I suspect without ever asking, "Why?" There is just a current naïve belief that a mission statement will magically lead to success or, at the very least, make the top managers look smart.

A heating and air-conditioning contractor handed me his card as we discussed the price of updating the system in my home. There on the bottom of his card was his company's mission statement. It said the company had "vision," was "dedicated to serving customers" and a few other nice things—all in about 18 words.

But the card didn't say what I really wanted to know: *Why* I should choose this company over any other heating and air conditioning outfit? The answer would be a *positioning message*.

This heating and air conditioning company and many others

proudly trumpet mission statements rather than focusing on the distinctiveness of the products or services they offer. They brag from their inward perspective rather than trying to understand my needs as a customer.

Most professional image and reputation management advisors I know counsel clients to spend minimal time on mission statements and only if they feel they must. Clients should instead focus quality time and real thought on positioning messages, where the words can create genuine competitive brand differentiation.

Why, you may ask, are positioning messages important when we seek to find more effective ways to communicate our messages and news to the media? Here is the answer: because one of our primary goals in approaching the news media is to communicate a subtle differentiating message about *our* organization to audiences reached by the media. We not only want to be reported on; we want also to be remembered. We want an audience to form a good impression about the value of your organization or perhaps the quality of your products.

What's the difference between a mission statement and a positioning message? There's a big difference. Here's a guide:

A mission statement tells people who are close to your organization where you want to go in a perfect world. It is idealistic and filled with words that tell people you are nice. It describes the future usually in terms of a quest for growth or a promise of unparalleled integrity. Who can argue with that? Yet mission statements do not get to the clear and specific differentiating reasons why a customer might hire your company over a competitor.

Let's take a look at a couple of examples of mission statements from not-for-profit conservation organizations. The mission statement for the National Wildlife Federation is "to protect wildlife for our children's future."

By comparison, the mission statement of the World Wildlife Fund, National Wildlife Federation's competitor, is, "The conservation of nature. Using the best available scientific knowledge and advancing that knowledge where we can, we work to preserve the diversity and abundance of life on Earth and the health of ecological systems."

While both mission statements are lofty and idealistic, they are general to the point of being dull. They lack the ability to competitively differentiate either group. Neither mission statement manages to tell an audience, "Yes, this phrase is specifically about National Wildlife Federation versus World Wildlife Fund." In fact, you could swap these statements between organizations and few of us would know the difference, and even fewer of us would care.

While I chose these mission statements at random, they are typical of most ones you will find. Mission statements don't, by definition, talk about where you are today or, more importantly, your competitive edge, but only what you hope to achieve.

Mission statements, like too many advertising, promotional, and press release claims, could apply just as easily to an organization's competitors.

You see, despite a common misperception, mission statements are intended to target and possibly inspire internal audiences—employees, stakeholders, boards of directors, and business partners. While the purpose of mission statements may be high-minded, they are by nature never very exciting, because they are future-focused. They do not create competitive positioning for an organization's image today. A mission statement is not a part of strategic communications—primarily because it does not address what's special about your organization versus that of a competitor.

On the other hand, a positioning message focuses on today and, if crafted carefully, will incisively leave an audience with a clear understanding of who you are and what is unique about your appealing business vision. It describes what is distinctive about your organization that will give it a competitive advantage today. It states how you wish to be perceived today.

Most important, a positioning message is a competitive differentiator that helps a customer choose you over someone else. It's a simple, plain language message, not a promotional slogan or tagline, that gets to the core of what's special about your organization. It is a pillar of strategic communications and media leadership.

Here's a story about one organization's costly misuse of a mission statement.

When I began advising leaders of 4-H on a major and ongoing initiative to reshape the image and brand of that national youth development organization, I walked into an environment that had only known mission statements and slogans. 4-H, like many other such groups, had changed their mission statement so often and had come up with slogans so frequently that the general, nondescript words had lost all meaning.

Incidentally, the 4-H organization had spent hundreds of tens of thousands of dollars on research and consultants and branding experts, and all they ever ended up with were slogans. One 4-H branding campaign, developed by the Advertising Council, promoted the slogan "Are You Into It?" The effort cost the youth group a fortune in advertising, and back-end testing revealed it had actually damaged the reputation of the 4-H brand.

Surveys conducted before and after the campaign revealed a 10 percent drop in respect for the organization's image as a result of the branding effort. It was found that the "Are You Into It?" phrase was so bland and non-descriptive that it painted 4-H as a boring organization with no special qualities or appeal. In other words, "Are You Into It?" communicated little value and was so general-sounding that it meant nothing. It demoted the 4-H reputation.

Yet 4-H's struggle to find its distinctive brand identification went much deeper. There are over 1,000 4-H related Web sites on the Internet, and, as a result, there are seemingly just about as many descriptions of 4-H. Many people know the brand and 4-H clover logo, but few have an understanding of what 4-H does as an organization. 4-H had become its own competition.

4-H leaders had invested hours revising their mission statement, and yet they continued to fail to attract new members and funding. In fact, both were on a decline. This decline can be attributed partly to the use of a mission statement in attempts to market 4-H to new audiences. By its very nature, the statement lacked differentiating characteristics that might show exciting reasons to choose 4-H over another youth organization.

4-H lacked a positioning message that would provide the chance to break through competitive clutter and recalibrate the 4-H brand to have greater influence to attract funding, members, and media.

I believed the solution could be found by talking with the youth of 4-H around America. The 4-H organization had previously spent a fortune on market research and advertising yet had never interviewed their number one and most important audience—the youth who belong to 4-H—to determine how they might describe the 4-H experience. Everything to that point had been from the perspective of adults, not youth. Grown-ups trying to figure out how to capture the attention of kids seldom works, as any parent knows.

My strategy was to find a way to describe the unique soul of 4-H in words that were clear and adjective-free and left no one out. In all of 4-H's branding efforts in the past, no one had ever gone out and interviewed the young people of the organization in such a detailed manner.

As I traveled from state to state chatting with groups of 4-H youth and listening to how they described the 4-H adventure, I heard the same words being used by many youths, whether they were in Madison, Georgia, or Davis, California. I call these words an organization's *common-thread words*.

4-H youth were using common-thread words like "community" and "young people." They said they were "learning" by working together in a mentoring environment with adults. What were they learning? I asked. "Leadership, citizenship, and life skills," they answered.

During my interviews I found it interesting that 4-H members often referred to their peers as "young people" as we discussed ways to describe 4-H to an outside audience. The adult leaders of the 4-H organization, by contrast, usually referred to the young people as "kids."

I listened to the youth of 4-H, and they told me, "4-H is a community of young people across America who are learning leadership, citizenship, and life skills."

The youth had defined one of the strongest positioning messages I had ever heard, and they had used distinctive words from *their* perspective, not from the viewpoint of adults talking about "kids."

The new positioning message said it all about America's oldest youth-development organization, and it said it in clear and simple language. It was an appealing message upon which to build a strategic communications campaign. Most of all, the message centered, for the first time ever, on the *value* of 4-H to young people. Previous attempts at messages had centered around the organization, which at the end of the day, no one really cared about.

Before long the entire organization was using the positioning message. It spread like wildfire. A young 4-H girl stood at a podium before the Governor of Indiana and 300 people to dedicate remodeled 4-H buildings at the Indiana State Fair, and she began by saying, "4-H is a community of young people across America who are learning leadership, citizenship, and life skills."

4-H youth put it on T-shirts. County agents use it on their e-mail signature lines. It is being used everywhere and at most levels of the organization. And the result is that wider audiences are becoming aware of the scope and impact of 4-H today in helping America's young people.

The 4-H organization, like countless other groups, had been caught up in a recent trend to improve and boost its brand when what it really needed was a distinctive way to describe itself in a single sentence.

Can you describe your business, organization, or product in a single sentence? Can you explain your endeavor in a few words that connects credibly with audiences that are important to you, including the news media? Is your organization speaking with a consistent "voice" that clearly and simply resonates favorably with audiences?

So many organizations hire branding firms that suggest all their problems will be solved with a new logo, slogan, and letterhead. That might help but it's not the complete solution. Reciting a new slogan will never impress journalists or get meaningful media coverage.

A clear and compelling positioning message is essential because it sets you apart from your competitors. And here's a tip: To sharpen your appeal, narrow your position. We cannot be all things to all people. To be successful, we must focus on one thing and be the best at it.

One thing, you say? Yes. Your organization might do many other things, but be recognized for excelling at one thing. Get people talking about that, and you will win competitively.

Remember all those "and more" businesses that couldn't figure out what they were? "Windows, Doors and More." "Yarns, Sewing and More." "Electronics, Hobbies and More."

Many of those places are gone simply because they failed to build a reputation of being outstanding in one area. They tried to be all things to all people.

Wal-Mart, you might argue, is one of those "and more" businesses. Not so. Even though they may sell just about everything imaginable, the company has for decades narrowly focused on one competitive message: "Always the Lowest Price. Always." That's Wal-Mart's positioning message, and they own it. In an ever-changing marketplace, they've been consistent, and they've won. Their promise has been fulfilled across America, and it has given them an enormous edge.

CHAPTER TWENTY-NINE

THE COST OF A FORGETTABLE SLOGAN

Let's take a look at the phenomena of slogans and why a host of branding companies would just love to sell you services to develop your new slogan.

Out of full disclosure, I admit that I've never been enthusiastic over the effectiveness of using slogans as a way to build awareness or create competitive success. Slogans generally are both inappropriate and useless when seeking media leadership.

Slogans, taglines, and catch phrases are, well, not really useful elements of normal and effective communication among people. Some people think that slogans will catch your attention, but I believe that most, while often clever-sounding, are also forgettable. These things certainly have no place in the practice of strategic communications.

When we, as human beings, communicate with each other—and through the media—we speak in complete sentences and complete thoughts, at least most of the time or with the exception of sending a text message by cell phone. Our children, of course, are another exception, especially when they are teenagers.

The best way to catch someone's attention is with a clear and plain language message that connects with and resonates favorably with the audience or person you are attempting to reach.

I was reading the *Washington Business Journal* and stopped at a story with a headline "Tourism Officials to Unveil New D.C. 'brand' research." The people who run the Washington, D.C., Convention &

Visitors Corporation had conducted new research to help the nation's capital to develop a new "brand." Halfway through the story was this line: "For nearly a decade, D.C. has used 'Washington, D.C.: The American Experience.'"

When I read that, my reaction ran from slight embarrassment to curiosity. Why had I not become aware of a slogan that has been used for nearly ten years?

Not to be deterred, I Googled, "The American Experience." On the first page of search results, Google listed sites related to the PBS television program of that name and to a Native American Web site, but nothing about Washington, D.C. A couple of Google pages later, I found a modest-looking and static Web site for Washington.org, the "official" site for tourism in the nation's capital.

Yet—and here was the really curious part—the Washington.org site failed to define the catch phrase, "The American Experience," or its relevance to the nation's capital. That is a primary pitfall of relying on slogans, taglines, and catch phrases—the words most often lack emotional or logical context.

Still feeling a little disappointed that I was not aware of Washington's tourism slogan, I conducted a straw poll of about 60 people who all have a close connection in one way or another with the nation's capital. I e-mailed one question which read, "With no prompting (or Googling), can you tell me what Washington, D.C.'s tourism promotion slogan is? Yes or No."

My random survey group included newspaper reporters, people at marketing and public affairs agencies in Washington, nationally known syndicated columnists, network and local journalists and broadcasters, a few secretaries, three attorneys, a realtor in Washington, local business owners, the leaders of trade associations and non-governmental organizations, and some friends. Only one person knew the slogan—just one. For everyone else, including me, our hometown's decade-old tourism slogan had missed us.

Now, you might respond that Washington's tourism slogan is intended for potential tourists around the country, not locals, and I would agree up to a point. But one of the easiest and most effective ways for any organization or city to market itself is from the inside out ... by getting people at home or within your organization excited first. Let the local folks (or your employees) help spread the news.

Organizations, like Washington's convention and tourism bureau, and major companies regularly pay hefty fees to branding firms for what might only amount to a new coat of paint, and a thin coat, at that. It's not surprising that the profit margin for client assignments at the largest branding firms often exceeds 60 percent.

On the other hand, many communications professionals have become skilled at developing positioning statements that help clients to more clearly reposition their image and, ultimately, their brand. A brand is not bought but rather earned through consistent words, deeds, and actions that communicate authentic value. Working with a communications agency is a quicker process and certainly more affordable for many clients. Public relations agencies also provide more effective implementation of a new positioning message.

Rather than slogans, I work with organizations on methods to begin to tell a story about the organization—using just a few plain language words, free of adjectives—that get to the heart of authentic value and special qualities of the organization. There is no need to tell the whole story; tell just enough to get an audience, including the media, to desire to know more.

A few carefully chosen and simple words can work wonders to differentiate an organization from competitors, leave a favorable impression and build a distinctive brand.

Apple, the innovative company that created the Macintosh computer and the widely popular iPhone and iPod, among many other cool items, is one of the best examples of a company that lives its brand image. When you purchase any Apple product, the company backs it up with a support network—online and telephone—that is easily understandable, even if your skills are new to the product. Apple's warranty is solutions-based, not seemingly avoidance-based as with their competitors, such as Dell.

Apple is a company that interacts with its customers. Visit the support section of Apple.com and you will easily find ways to e-mail your question or join an online forum. If you send an e-mail, a response comes promptly.

The Cupertino, California, based company is renown for reflecting its brand promise in everything it does. So, it is no surprise that Apple has made many friends, including in the news media and the New Media community.

When Apple has good news, it is trumpeted by the media. On the other hand, when Apple has a problem, as all companies do, the media is often more understanding. This isn't about having a nifty looking logo that's become somewhat of a cult symbol; it is about living the company's image and reputation in everything it does. In the computer manufacturing industry, Apple is pretty much alone on that score.

How does Apple talk about itself to the media? With plain language words and phrases, and no technology jargon. Apple is one of those rare tech companies that recognizes that its primary business is customer service. The company has also mastered the talent of connecting with customers about the value and benefits of using Apple products. Little wonder that Apple's sales soar.

Apple's positioning statement is fluid, conversational, and adaptive. Here's an example: "Apple … reinvented the personal computer in the 1980s with the Macintosh, and today continues to lead the industry in innovation with its award-winning computers, OS X operating system and spearheading the digital media revolution."

The company's news releases are free of those *about* paragraphs that amount to little more than cheap self-promotion. Apple is one of those few companies that understands the *about* section compromises the journalistic integrity of news releases. Besides, if someone wants more information, they can check the company's Web site.

I suppose that years as a communications strategist has taught me that slogans and taglines will never replace authentic messages that seem to reach inside and connect with our emotions.

But, while on the subject, let me share a couple of exceptions. A few slogans have endured over the years because they share the common essential element of being able to emotionally and logically connect with our primal needs or desires.

"The American Experience" failed miserably for Washington, D.C., because it lacked relevance and did not reflect any true quality of contemporary Washington. Besides, PBS Television had used it first.

The introduction of the 1960s Virginia Slims cigarette brand brought with it the "You've Come a Long Way Baby" slogan that was aimed at women. Even though cigarette advertising is now banned on television, the slogan lived on for a while in pop lexicon.

"GE brings good things to life" suggests something warm and cozy but what does it really mean about the conglomerate that manufactures light bulbs and jet aircraft engines and owns NBC, among other things?

I must admit that I do have a favorite slogan. It is, "Virginia is for Lovers." These four words work so well to evoke imagery and emotion because they are as much a positioning statement as slogan. Someone can begin a media interview or make a speech by saying, "Virginia is for lovers …" and then explain why.

"Virginia is for Lovers" was created by a trio of tourism and advertising pros in Richmond, Virginia, in 1969 and is still recognized widely, even though there has been a movement to officially retire the words. Incidentally, there are many advertising people around the country who claim to have created the line—including one ad guy who was a child in 1969 when the slogan debuted.

Maybe it was because the timing was right in 1969 when the slogan was launched. Even though the United States was mired in a war in Vietnam, love was in the air and a common theme—Erich Segal's book "Love Story" was a bestseller as well as Jacqueline Susann's "The Love Machine." It was the time of Woodstock when 300,000 young people gathered for a weekend of peace, love, music, and drugs.

The Virginia tourism people say that part of the mystique of the slogan is that it has meant many things to different people. It connects on an individual level. When I hear the phrase, "Virginia is for Lovers," it congers up positive images in my mind of the state where I grew up.

On the other hand, there are thousands of slogans that never quite work even though organizations hire branding experts and invest significant resources.

My best advice for creating distinctive positioning for your organization is to begin crafting the story about how customers or clients benefit from the authentic value your organization delivers. Don't talk about yourself because no one cares. Talk about the benefits and value people get from what your organization does. Focus on a way to explain that story in just a couple of clear and direct sentences. Get right to the point.

Remember my example earlier in this book of the message that the youth of the national 4-H organization came up with and that said it all: "4-H is a community of young people across America who are learning leadership, citizenship, and life skills." The simple sentence has worked to distinctively capture the special value of the 4-H experience for young people.

CHAPTER THIRTY

WHEN A GREAT IMAGE
GETS RESULTS

My strategic communications agency worked with the CEO and marketing people at Learjet headquarters in Wichita, Kansas, on their challenge to introduce a new business jet, the Learjet 45. Rollouts of new corporate jets had become so commonplace in Wichita that even the hometown daily newspaper, the *Wichita Eagle*, no longer saw any news value in sending a reporter or photographer out to cover them.

I discussed our situation with noted photographer and photojournalist Ed Lallo, whom I had hired to get publicity pictures of the new business jet. Lallo had never before worked on an aviation project and came to town with fresh ideas on how to get a winning photo of the Learjet 45. His concept was both daring and somewhat dangerous: to get the then-Learjet CEO, Brian Barents, to stand on top of a Learjet 45 for a photo session. My job was to talk Barents into the stunt, and Barents didn't let me down.

We were out before dawn one morning with a dew-covered Learjet 45 on a remote tarmac of Wichita's airport with two cherry-picker cranes—one to hoist Barents up on top of the jet, and the other to position Lallo, with all his camera gear, right above the nose of the jet.

I stood in the background, noting that Barents was wearing slick-soled Italian loafers while standing on the curved and still dew-moistened top of the jet, about 20 feet in the air. There were no safety nets, and he stayed in position only through his own nerve and calm balance. No trick photography … it was the real thing.

photo by Ed Lallo

Lallo rapid-fired both of his cameras and got the picture he wanted within 60 seconds. Barents was carefully retrieved from his dangerous perch, and the photo shoot was complete. The next step was a quick trip to a local one-hour photo lab to check the negatives (this event happened just before professional quality digital cameras became available). Next, we were on to the local Associated Press office where, through Lallo's personal contacts, a photo was digitally scanned and transmitted to AP headquarters in New York.

From there the photo went to newspapers nationwide and around the world on the AP PhotoWire, along with a caption I wrote that began, "On Top of the Industry—Brian Barents, Learjet president and CEO, feels like he's on top of the world with the rollout of the first Learjet 45, an aircraft that redefines light business jet aircraft." The caption went on to trumpet the debut of the Learjet 45 and a couple of the aircraft's special features.

Our photo with caption was picked up by more than 800 newspapers and magazines across America and globally with a combined readership of 34 million people, making it one of the most successful photo promotions in the history of corporate aviation. And yes, one of those papers was even the *Wichita Eagle*, which ran the photo in the middle of the front page, above the fold, the next morning. Overnight one imaginative photo broke the mold and set a new standard for how business aircraft were promoted through the general news media.

All of a sudden the phones at Learjet were ringing. The company had instantly connected with the pulse of a whole new market of potential customers: wealthy individuals who could afford the price tag. These individuals, many of them software and technology *nouveau riche*, wanted an affordable business jet to get places quickly. One single yet extraordinary photograph got the attention of new audiences and favorably changed the brand image of the company.

Yet until that time, individual customers had mostly been an elusive audience for Learjet, because they had never before owned a business aircraft and did not read the aviation trade magazines where Learjet advertised; consequently, the company had not figured out how to get their attention.

The media has always loved imaginative, timely, and relevant photos—unusual subjects, action, the unexpected, people doing crazy things. A "Wow!"-type of picture that people will rave about. The difference today is an even greater desire by the media—all kinds of media—to use appealing photos that will entice readers and viewers.

"Eye candy" is what many news photographers and editors call great pictures. You see them all the time in *National Geographic* and *People* magazines: photos taken by skilled photographers who are always looking for appealing and clever angles to tell the story. For world-class photographers, like Ed Lallo, capturing those attention-getting and memorable photos that tell a compelling story in a single image is a talent that seems to come naturally. Even when words seem to fail to adequately tell the story, a great photo can make news, enhance brand awareness and enrich your future.

CHAPTER THIRTY-ONE

THE VALUE OF
GETTING ACQUAINTED

A desk side briefing to get acquainted with a reporter can be one of the best ways for a media savvy executive to generate initial interest in his or her company or organization. It's particularly effective because the tactic is not widely used by many public relations practitioners. If you play your cards right and if some basic rules are followed, the desk side session can lead to a good story.

The concept is to schedule an informal meeting with a reporter who covers your industry or business, get an understanding of the reporter's needs, and talk briefly about your organization or issue. The objective of a desk side briefing is to lay the groundwork for a possible future story, provide editorial direction, and build a relationship. It is not to ask for a story.

Let's say that a few journalists have written about your company, product, or service, but it would be a major coup to have a story appear in the media.

Despite numerous calls by your communications people to the correct reporter, nothing is happening. It's going nowhere. Phone calls are either not being returned, or the reporter has told you that while the story seems interesting, it lacks a good news angle. That's a polite way of saying the reporter perceives your outfit as no big deal and unworthy of his or her time.

The more obvious and predictable approach used by PR people when pitching a story—perhaps to a reporter they've never before met—

has not worked. So we need to try something else to get attention. It's time for ... drum roll, please ... a *desk side briefing*.

Here's how it works.

The concept is to get the CEO or a leading executive at a company or organization in front of the right reporter for a brief, early morning background meeting. The desk side is *not* billed as an interview, but as a quick background briefing. Ideally, you should meet the reporter informally for about 30 minutes before his or her normal work starting time, and—this is very important—keep the meeting shorter than the time requested.

Before attempting to schedule a desk side briefing, assign a communications person to do some research about the reporter to make certain you are contacting the right one. Take a look at some of his or her recent work so you can mention it in your conversation and compliment that work. Look for areas of overlap or connection between what this reporter has previously written and your potential story.

All reporters have a particular *beat*, or range of topics they cover, often defined by their personal interests. For example, Thomas Friedman at the *New York Times* has become one of the country's foremost opinion-leaders on the Middle East because of his interest in the region; Dan Balz is national political correspondent at the *Washington Post*; and Jackie Northam covers national security at National Public Radio. You get the picture.

E-mail can be a good way to snag the attention of a reporter, especially with a clever approach, said Marcus Chan at the *San Francisco Chronicle*.

"The best e-mail pitches (or more accurately, the ones I actually read) are the ones that sound like they're coming from a regular reader; they offer meaningful and specific comments to published stories, and often, it's not until the very end that I realize it's a PR pitch. But those are the ones I read."

Crafting an effective e-mail pitch that catches a reporter's attention can reach the level of, well, of a form of art.

Being concise is key when it comes to asking a journalist to meet about a possible story idea. You must create a brief, focused, alluring, and—most of all—low-key pitch in order to schedule the meeting. Once you've got the right journalist, you need to hook his or her interest—the quicker the better. Your chances diminish the more you talk. Whether you send an e-mail, leave a message on voice mail, or actually get the reporters on the phone live, get right to the point with an action plan. Tell the reporter you have a possible story in mind and why you think he or she might be interested, briefly referencing something similar he or she has written. OK, I will say it: Play to their egos.

When you get the attention of the right reporter, don't waste his or her time with trivial politeness unless you are personal pals. Avoid beginning a call or e-mail with "How are you today?" or the insipid phrase "What's up?" Get right to the point.

Then do something unusual: Do not pitch or ask for a story. That's too predictable. Say something like, "My purpose for contacting you is not about a story, but rather to provide a brief backgrounder about our organization, which is in the industry you regularly cover."

You are not pitching a story but merely seeking a meeting to provide background. This unique approach implies exclusiveness. It merits a reporter meeting you before work to at least listen. Underscore to the reporter that you know the importance of their work demands and, besides, you—as an executive and leader—have a limited amount of time as well, so an early-morning meeting would work best. Remember, it's an informal meeting.

Here are some ground rules:

- Do not send information prior to the desk side meeting for a couple of reasons. First, it begins to feel like a predictable story pitch. Second, you may be sending the wrong material. Third, the reporter is likely to lose or misplace the stuff sent in advance, which could create an awkward moment when you arrive and the reporter can't find it. Only send advance material if the reporter specifically insists on it, and then only send what they request —nothing more.

- Resist the traditional public relations urge to impress the reporter with reams of news media kits and a load of other stuff. When you go to a desk side, intentionally take only the briefest supporting material with you—preferably no brochures, no media kit. In that way, you create an opportunity to have personalized follow-up contact with the reporter by providing specific material the reporter wants as a result of the meeting. That not only keeps the reporter focused on your potential story, it also works to build a relationship of trust and confidence with the reporter and boosts your chances that a story will happen.

- Remember the purpose of the desk side briefing: It is not an interview, but a briefing; and second, you are not asking the reporter to do a story. It's an informal chance to meet—for the first time—a journalist who can be important to your organization. It is *relationship building*.

- During the meeting, focus on one or two main messages. Avoid making the reporter's eyes glaze over by talking about too many issues. Focus on a couple of competitive advantages that may complement the reporter's past articles.

- At the conclusion of a desk side briefing, define an informal follow-up plan. Ask the reporter if there is any material you can send that might be helpful. Find out the best way you can stay in touch. Via e-mail? Phone?

- Treat the desk side briefing as a bonding opportunity to develop a working relationship with the journalist. Thank the reporter for his or her time. Show sincere appreciation. And do not—ever—ask for a story. Even if the reporter suggests a possible story, say you would be happy if the conversation led to that, but you just appreciated chatting with him or her for a few minutes.

Once I took a CEO for an early morning desk side briefing with a reporter and, when the meeting concluded, the executive could not resist the urge, even though I had cautioned him against asking, "When are you going to do a story?" The reporter understandably looked ambushed and deceived, and, clearly, he had been by the CEO.

The desk side meeting had been scheduled with the understanding that it was neither an interview nor an implied commitment to do a story. It was a unique opportunity to meet with a reporter who had or might have otherwise said no to a traditional interview. We had broken the ground rules of the meeting. It was like breaking a promise.

On the other hand, desk side briefings can be very effective. Newspaper columnist and HDNet television senior correspondent Greg Dobbs told me about a meeting he had with a public relations representative regarding the trend toward just-in-time manufacturing, a process of efficiently managing often costly inventories to allow more competitive pricing of products.

"She made me aware of a concept growing in popularity in American industry," Dobbs said. "When she had my attention, she then offered her client to serve as my example in a feature story. It worked. Win-Win.

"She turned me on to the concept, and then, by getting me in her client's door, earned her pay."

The *New York Post's* Linda Stasi cautions, "We know and you know that you're there to sell something I probably don't want, so be upfront about it. Never, never oversell or lie. If you do, remember, the reporter is the one with the last word—and that word will be in ink and read (hopefully) by many people."

I received an e-mail from a public relations person in the state of Qatar in the Middle East who said a desk side briefing may be ideal in a perfect situation, but his primary media contacts are far-flung around the world, making in-person meetings nearly impossible. I understand his challenge, but the objectives are to get to know a journalist at some level of familiarity, work to establish trust, and build a professional relationship.

Yes, a face-to-face meeting is preferable, but the concept also will work through a telephone conversation with follow-up e-mail contact, and the same rules apply.

A desk side briefing—in whatever form it takes—is a resourceful way to get the attention of an important reporter and establish a productive working relationship that will pay off and help you get an edge on your competitors.

CHAPTER THIRTY-TWO

A TIME AND A PLACE FOR NEWS RELEASES

Ask journalists or anyone in today's media, and they will freely admit that press releases seldom result in a story. News releases ... press releases ... whatever you call them, are one of the least effective ways to communicate with today's media, as I have mentioned earlier.

The compulsiveness of companies and organizations to send out news releases is most often counter-productive to the wishes of executives who simply want to get the media's attention on an important issue.

When I spoke with Brian Lamb, the founder and chief executive officer of C-SPAN, he said news releases are the worst way to communicate with the media. "Public relations people," he said, "simply do not understand that the media is certainly not driven by and generally does not care about news releases."

News releases simply are not the way news stories happen in today's highly competitive and New Media world.

There are, of course, a few exceptions—such as releases mandated by due diligence requirements to announce financial news. There is also a style of releases that reflect a savvier, most sophisticated approach to managing news through storytelling. Yet, the vast majority of releases fall far short of that objective.

Apple is about the only company that has mastered the technique of actually delivering legitimate news stories through their releases, and they achieve outstanding results because of it. Apple's communications people know that reporters are paid to write stories; so, their news releases are actual stories. But they are the exception—the rare exception—rather than the rule.

Yet, aside from real storytelling that trumpets real news or financial announcements, the media seldom pays attention or cares about releases.

A media savvy top executive is the only person who can stop this perpetually bad habit of so many companies to issue irrelevant news releases that are not news. When organizations stop talking about themselves and start talking in terms of stories that appeal to the media, they reap significant increases in media attention.

Sadly, the vast majority of news releases, however, are little more than self-serving promotion and thinly disguised attempts at sales marketing. Don't believe me? Well, then, explain that compulsive habit of adding an "about…" paragraph at the end of each news release?

It started during the tech boom of the 1990s when startups had CEOs and marketing people—not communicators—writing news releases, which they saw as an opportunity to turn a news release into a sales brochure. In other words, "Since we don't have any real news to announce, let's issue a release to make up stuff and brag about how great we are!" When the attorneys got their hands on the releases, they recognized such bravado as "b-s" and insisted that releases contain safe harbor statements that essentially said that nothing in the release is true and the company has no memory of ever having claimed it and it's not their fault.

Some public relations agencies know that releases are largely a waste of time but crank them out nonetheless at the behest of clients. After all, sending out releases means additional billable hours.

Publicity people in America flood the news media with unknown thousands of news releases each year. There's an erroneous belief—but one that's alive nonetheless—that if you send a release to as many reporters as possible, it will mystically increase in importance. Hence, the popularity of news release distribution services—such as, PR Newswire and BusinessWire—which each distribute more a thousand releases each day. Pile on the countless news releases from a growing number of online press releases distribution services, and those from PR agencies, companies, governments, and organizations e-mail, fax, and mail to the media, and the total amount is overwhelming.

It is a myth that sending news releases to thousands of reporters will make a difference. There is no alchemy magic. Quite the contrary, you just might get tagged as an annoyance.

Here is the reality: Most news releases are not read or are ignored. Unsolicited, irrelevant and meaningless news releases—the overwhelming bulk of releases e-mailed to newsrooms—are the number one complaint of journalists about the PR business.

A PR person sent a single news release to about 1,300 reporters and editors. I learned about it because an editor I know shared the e-mail with me after counting the names in the "To" line. He stopped counting at 1,300 e-mail addresses. The sender hadn't bothered to hide the 1,300 in the "Bcc" line, but simply just mindlessly blasted out his news release with all the names revealed. The amount of space those 1,300 names consumed in an e-mail was massive. Incidentally, he left the "Subject" line empty even though that's an important place to try to get a journalist's attention.

Such practices are not limited to a single PR person. The White House communications office during the administration of George W. Bush was notorious for sending out releases with thousands of e-mail addresses revealed in the "To" line, an aggravating practice for journalists who check e-mail on small screens of Blackberry devices and would wear a callus on their thumb just to scroll to the actual content.

The problem of mass e-mailing of news releases has reached such proportions that news organizations now actively work to block releases in special spam filters to prevent the sheer volume of them from overwhelming the e-mail inboxes of reporters and editors.

There is a rising tide of concern that the public relations industry could be labeled among the top spammers on the Internet. PR's volume of blind and unsolicited pitches to the news media via e-mail is already staggering, out of control, and growing, fueled by a proliferation of online services that promise to deliver your press release to thousands of journalists by e-mail, even though such an approach is rarely effective.

News releases are an overused crutch in the public relations business. Many executives and public relations people criticize the news media for not paying attention to their organizations but then rely solely on issuing a never-ending string of poorly written news releases—which seldom have any relevance or news value and are often self-serving sales promotion drivel, a holdover from a bygone era.

While a news release unquestionably can get the attention of a reporter or editor, it's not often that a release by itself results in a news story, except at smaller, free or weekly newspapers.

It's fairly rare to see a news release that contains legitimate, balanced news. Yet many public relations people—and their bosses—think that all they need to do is issue a release, and the media will come running. It doesn't work that way.

Veteran journalists generally have become wary of trivial fluff or blatantly commercial self-promotion under the "news release" banner.

"When I get a news release telling me of a new hire, or burying the lead of a plausible story," said Greg Dobbs, correspondent and anchor of "World Report" on HDNet, "then anything else I get from them feels like too much. Knowing my priorities means, among other things, knowing when I might use their information and knowing when I might not ... which is 'when' they shouldn't send it in the first place."

Effective news releases must be just that—news. Not fluff, not a sales promotion, certainly not "about" your company—but legitimate news. As I have mentioned throughout this book, savvy communications today requires the skill of storytelling. Even a news release must present *a story*.

George Lewis, who covers technology for NBC News, told me, "one piece of advice to PR people when pitching tech stories: tell reporters in ordinary English why the gadget or service they're promoting will make ordinary people's lives better. Don't use terms like 'comprehensive multitasking solution' because that sort of yadda-yadda-yadda makes my eyes glaze over.

"And, if you can't figure out how your product will positively impact ordinary people, don't bother pitching it. And remember, we don't do infomercials for your client. We're covering trends more than gadgets, and your client's product may be lumped in with the competition's if we do the story."

Another piece of valuable advice from reporters: Figure out how to clearly describe the distinctiveness or value of your organization and what it does in one sentence. Not an elevator speech because that takes too long in today's world but one sentence, but about 20 words max.

If there is one thing for an executive to know about news releases, it is that people in the media are paid to find new, fresh, and original news stories. News releases are the absolute antithesis of what today's media wants or needs. Why should a journalist care when you are sharing your so-called news with their competitors? That's why releases are the least effective method of getting the media's attention. In fact, news releases have become a major annoyance to the media.

Nonetheless, if you still feel the urge to issue a news release, identify a timely and relevant purpose, as well as a story angle. What are you announcing, why is it important to your audiences and who cares? Stick to one purpose and seek to establish credibility through candor and openness.

Use a news release to capture the media's interest about a possible story and make them want to learn more about the subject or issue. How do you achieve that?

Here are some ways:

- *Send it to the right people in the media:* PR people need to get a grip on the lazy habit of sending releases to the wrong person or carpet-bombing thousands of people in the media, using blast e-mail services. Such practices make them look incompetent, which clearly they are.

- *Take a journalist's perspective*: Is your news release actually timely news that the media might find interesting, or is it self-serving fluff? Develop a legitimate news story in the news release—something the media will find appealing.

- *Cut to the chase*: Why should anyone care about the information you are releasing? Get to the bottom line in the first sentence, then provide background in the body of the release. Isn't that how news stories are crafted by the media? They write a headline that catches your eye, then provide enough in the first sentence or two to whet your appetite. If you want to know more, read on.

- *Be timely*: This is one essential element of news. Develop timely news releases.

- *Keep the news release to one page*: You heard me … one page. I assure you that when you go beyond one page, the media's attention drops exponentially, regardless of what you have to say.

- *Give the media an easy way to contact you and learn more*: Give them your phone numbers and make sure you answer; don't let their call go to voicemail.

When developing a news release, remember that most releases are rarely, if ever used, so be realistic and imaginative. Use news releases as working tools for journalists to provide clarity on your messages and focus for what you have to say. Good news releases can be valuable weapons in the communications arsenal.

For example, use a news release to achieve targeted awareness of several media outlets for exclusive industry or financial trend research that your organization may have commissioned. That approach positions you as an industry leader.

Another example is to use a news release to provide clarity and transparency to a complex issue. In other words, use a release to cut through jargon, cluttered messages, and contentious arguments, and to deliver credible understanding, using plain language.

Use a news release to help deliver messages intended to right a wrong.

A news release is intended to announce credible news—clear, compelling, and straightforward. Avoid overworked promotion phrases and jargon, such as, "Ramping up to provide mission critical assistance to ProSupport customers." Sales promotion terminology in news releases seldom rings with authentic credibility and appeal.

Paper the news media too many times with trivial promotion or sales pieces under the guise of a "news release," and you will not only kill their interest in your organization when you have something real to announce, but you will drive them to your competitor.

Many companies are guilty of having cranked out meaningless news releases. The practice is more often the case than the exception. Yet the news media is not driven by and generally doesn't care about news releases, to echo the words of C-SPAN's Brian Lamb.

Effective strategic communications in today's world is about having solid contacts among journalists and knowing how to present a story idea to the right person at the right time.

"I find that 90 percent of PR people do a really poor job," said Barbara Bradley Hagerty of National Public Radio. "They pitch stories with no angles, just kind of pitch randomly. They don't think through that journalists need a *news* peg. They don't offer specifics for sources to back up the story or how we can cover it quickly."

"Rarely is a story pitched right," according to Richard Danbury of BBC Television News in London. "I suppose a key here is to know the journalists' preoccupations and pitch accordingly. When I was a lawyer, I was taught the golden rule of advocacy: know thy tribunal."

In the important tribunal of public opinion, how you are seen, perceived, and talked about when you make news—or attempt to make news—can make all the difference between recognition as a winner or standing in the shadows as a runner-up. The distinctive style by which you practice strategic communications—the approaches you take and the words you use—will make the difference. It's all up to you.

So, here's the takeaway:

First, blast or indiscriminate distribution of unsolicited e-mails rarely works in either getting the attention of a journalist or resulting in a story. What's more, companies are actually teaching smart spam software to recognize more and more of the materials of public relations as spam. Hence, news releases are becoming seen as online spam. Sorry, but that is the reality in today's media world.

Second, the news business has gotten so fiercely competitive that reporters are mandated to find exclusive and appealing stories that have not appeared elsewhere. News releases go out to everyone so why would a reporter who wants to keep a job bother to touch it?

Third, today's style of effective strategic communications is relationship-based. The most effective PR people smartly build trusted relationships with only the right reporters and share story ideas, one-on-one.

Here's my advice: Forget news releases. Let me restate what I wrote in the first chapter of this book:

Protecting a reputation begins with understanding the implications and potential cost of not protecting a reputation.

Protecting an organization's reputation ultimately is the

responsibility of the executive at the top, so isn't it time to roll up your shirt (or blouse) sleeves, and master all the strategies, tactics, tools, and nuance that make for a media savvy leader?

- Get to know reporters who cover your business or organization on a first-name basis. Chances are there are just a few.

- Build trust and an open exchange of ideas.

- Establish yourself as a regular resource of tips and information, which gives you an opportunity to stay in contact with the journalists.

- Develop the skill of communicating your organization's vision and news through an engaging form of storytelling.

Then, whether you have legitimate news or need to manage a crisis, pick up the phone and talk with the right person in the media. That's how the best stories happen. That's how to manage today's media.

CHAPTER THIRTY-THREE

FORGET LISTS; FIND INFLUENCERS

There's a popular misconception in the public relations industry that the larger the media list—the more names on it—the better. While this might seem like too gritty of a detail for any executive to be bothered with, take a closer look.

The issue is about a common myth among many inexperienced PR people that is counter-productive in today's media world and will adversely impact not just media coverage, but your organization's reputation. A media savvy leader wants to achieve razor-sharp impact for an organization's messages. The out-of-date shotgun tactic does not work.

As stated previously, I've found many corporate communications departments, especially those within large companies, to compulsively shovel out news releases indiscriminately to as many people in the media as possible. Quantity over quality is the conventional wisdom.

Part of the reason is lack of media contacts; part is that they may not have any other ideas. And, part is fear that they are not doing their job until half the people on the planet receive an unsolicited spam e-mail press release from your organization.

In fact, an entire cottage industry of service companies that offer media lists has sprung up. Thousands and thousands of media names are provided for a price. Google the search terms, "press release distribution service," and you will get more than seven million references.

Vocus, one of the numerous online services that provide media relations support, boasts "access to a global media directory of over 400,000 unique journalists, updated daily." Holy cow! Am I impressed? Certainly not.

Vocus, incidentally, started out as a couple of software guys who had written a contact-sharing product for the medical industry. When that failed to meet expectations, they turned their sights to a service to aggregate and manage massive lists of media contacts for PR people who—lacking experience in working directly with the media—had fallen into the bad and ineffective habit of blindly sending out press materials in the hope someone might be interested.

In speaking with many communications people, I have never heard anyone suggest that Vocus, Cision, or any other mass distribution services for press releases actually resulted in generating news stories on a sustained basis. As you will see later in this chapter, there is a use for the services companies such as these offer, just be sure to use their lists discriminately.

Today's style of approaching the media involves narrowing your focus and resources to the areas in which you will have the maximum impact. That means reducing your media list and concentrating on those reporters who can best cover your organization.

Jennifer Barrett of *Newsweek* spoke for most journalists when she said, "It would be more effective for a PR person to concentrate their efforts on a couple dozen key reporters and get to know what topics they like and what they tend to write about most, and build trust with them, rather than to spend their time sending out dozens of generic e-mails to reporters and hoping someone bites.

"When I'm in a crunch, I go first to those PR people whom I trust and I know I can rely on to get the right sources quickly. I literally have a short list of about a half-dozen PR people to whom I turn regularly for story sources."

Barrett's advice is brilliant for people who are responsible for media relations: become a trusted media source. Build relationships with journalists, as you have heard many times in this book, and become a credible source.

Roy Gutman, *Newsday*'s foreign editor who won the Pulitzer Prize for investigative reporting, concurs. "Be the database for the issue you support, and don't seek credit, even for a job well done."

"If you have a genuine story," Gutman shared with me, "openness, readiness to connect a reporter with the authentic voices of the story, and general assistance is truly welcome."

Using a shotgun approach to get the media's attention by sending news releases and stories randomly to as many reporters and news organizations as possible seldom works, can cost a ton of money, and often tends to hurt your reputation rather than help it.

It's always important to maintain an up-to-date list of media contacts, but quality of contacts is far more important than quantity. Many public relations people are insecure and concerned they might miss sending something to someone important in the news media, but it's not necessary to pepper a whole newsroom with your releases.

The news media is inundated every day by too much publicity stuff that's too poorly targeted. In some cases, the same media materials are sent to multiple reporters and editors, regardless of whether they cover the issue or not. Some of it is sent to reporters at organizations for which they haven't worked for years. Yet in other cases, the right reporter doesn't receive a copy.

An important element of effectively reaching out to the media is targeting the right journalists with a story angle that might capture their interest.

The single most valuable piece of advice offered by Scott Simon, host on National Public Radio, is, "Know who you are calling. I am amazed at the number of calls I get from people representing books (like *100 Ways to Grow a Great Rutabaga!*), music CDs, or people that no one who listens to our program should think we would be interested in. We don't keep our show a secret; several million people listen. Before you call us, you should try to put yourself among them, at least for a week or two, to make a better informed presentation."

So how do you start crafting a media list that will achieve results? Even though you may be leading an organization or managing a group of professionals, it is important to know the seemingly gritty details of how to effectively win friends in the media.

Stop for a minute and think about the number of reporters who have written anything about your organization or business in the last year. You will generally find that this is no more than a handful.

Of course, if you work for a high-profile company with many consumer products and services—such as Microsoft, Apple, Coca-Cola, GE, or Colgate—it may be a different story. But even then it is likely that only a few reporters will follow your outfit on a regular basis and do the substantive reporting that influences other journalists.

As senior vice president for the corporate image and reputation management practice at Edelman Public Relations, I encountered the head of communications for a major aerospace company who had never bothered, in several years on the job, to learn the name of one single reporter who covered his company. Not one. He told me, flatly, that he hired us to deal with the news media because he didn't want to be bothered. Such an attitude is blatantly irresponsible, and it's not surprising that the fellow subsequently lost his job.

When it came right down to it, we found that only about eight or ten journalists covered his company's particular slice of the whole aerospace company on a regular basis, and what they reported carried broad influence throughout the aerospace industry and even to Wall Street.

I'd be willing to bet that for most corporations, there are fewer than a dozen reporters who really count when it comes to getting out a story about the organization, and it is the job of the person in charge of working with the media to establish and skillfully nurture relationships with these reporters.

And while you are making contacts with reporters and editors, don't overlook the wire services. The stories written by reporters at The Associated Press, Reuters, and Bloomberg appear in hundreds of newspapers. Those reporters are *media influencers*. They set the tone for others and they are critical to your organization. Find them and court them. Communicate with them personally on a regular basis, never through an intermediary service. Get to know them and what they need and seek in story ideas.

Here's a checklist for creating an effective top-tier media list:

- *Get online and find out who writes about your organization.* Use an online news retrieval service, such as ProQuest or LexisNexis, to find the newspaper and magazine stories written about your organization in the last year. These archiving services provide access, usually with a nominal charge, to thousands of current periodicals and newspapers, many updated daily and containing full-text articles that date back to the mid-to-late 1980s. You want to find stories in which a reporter invested some time and wrote a substantial piece of journalism about your organization or business arena. Make a list of those reporters and pay particular attention to the ones who have written thoughtful pieces about your company. Put them at the top of the list.

- *Invest in resource materials.* If your budget will allow it, consider the services of a respected news media contact service, such as Cision or Burrelle's. They will provide the basic information about specific media, reporters, beats, and contact information. But don't let them do your job for you. The news business is transient. Reporters move around a lot, either within their company or between other news organizations. Consequently, there's a chance that today's accurate media contact information will be outdated tomorrow. As mentioned previously, use these lists discriminately and as a starting point to find appropriate journalists.

- *Make phone calls.* Get the latest and most accurate media contact information. Reach out to news organizations that are important to you. If your online research hasn't turned up good results, no problem. Simply make a list of media that you believe might be interested in reporting your story or, more important, where you would like to see your story appear, and give them a call. Let's say, for example, that you work for a not-for-profit group that develops after school programs to help urban youth and you want to generate media coverage in cities like Philadelphia, Boston, and Atlanta. It's easy. Begin by calling the metro or local news assignment desks of the local media in those cities. Ask who covers education or inner city issues and speak with that reporter. Most journalists are eager to know of an interesting new story. A phone call to a news organization often leads to the most valuable kind of contact. Personal contact is a key step in getting ready for a story pitch to the media.

- *Test the water.* If in doubt about whether you have a news story, ask when you call a news organization for updated contact details. There is nothing wrong with calling a reporter whom you have identified as being interested in your organization and saying, "I think I've got the elements of a good story for you, but I need a little help giving it focus." You will be surprised at the helpful guidance you will receive.

- *Keep it professional.* Find out how specific journalists prefer to be contacted about future news from your business and get all their contact details. Remember, it's not a conversation. Effective media outreach is a ritual. You have called the reporter to plant the seeds of initial interest and to ask them how they wanted to be contacted about stories. Your goal is to present a story idea in such a seductive way as to elicit a response from the journalist to learn more.

- *Update.* Even the most effective media lists don't last forever. Reporters change jobs and assignments. Make it a practice to update your entire media list at least every quarter. This will be easy to do because of the contact information you will have collected. If someone doesn't respond, give him or her a call. If there's still no response, assume there's been a change, and call that department at the newspaper to make inquiries and gather fresh contact details. In my strategic communications consulting practice in which I work with numerous reporters all the time, I routinely get e-mails from journalists who are changing jobs or assignments.

Effective relationships with the news media are not something to take casually or pass along to a third party, such as a public relations agency, unless you are absolutely assured that contacts will be professionally managed.

An increasing number of leading executives are taking an active role in communicating news and their vision for their organizations directly with established contacts in the media.

National Public Radio's Barbara Bradley Hagerty counsels

executives to "figure out who you should get in touch with and go to that person directly. Work with that right person as opposed to contacting everyone. That's annoying."

The best and most responsible media coverage is usually the result of developing an ongoing professional relationship with a journalist who is interested in your story.

The leaders who gain influence and get results in today's competitive world have established valuable relationships and trust with the media, and the rewards are frequently incalculable.

CHAPTER THIRTY-FOUR

BE CLEVER AND BOLD

I knew a public relations person in Denver who felt the only way to get the media's attention was to do something flashy. So when sending out a news release on behalf of her clients, she would also fill the envelope with glittery confetti—the metallic stuff that's impossible to vacuum up from a carpet. I suppose she didn't feel that the content of her client's news releases could stand up alone, so she wanted to make sure her mailings were noticed.

They were noticed all right: After making the mistake of opening her confetti-filled envelopes a couple of times, reporters and editors just pitched the whole thing, unopened, into the nearest trash can. Rather than gaining recognition as a credible public relations person, she developed a reputation as a prankster.

Everyone, including journalists, enjoys imaginative new ideas that get their attention. But if your idea only distracts the recipients, or annoys them by filling their carpets with confetti, you've lost the battle.

Unfortunately, in the public relations business—which should be distinguished by clever thinking—imaginative and new ideas and approaches for effective communication are few and far between. The business is instead driven by the same dull, worn-out tactics over and over ... and over.

There is nothing wrong with trying to get the media's attention through a small gift so long as it's relevant to the story and not something expensive or valuable that might compromise a journalist's integrity or get them in hot water with their company's rules about accepting gifts. It's easy enough to find out what those rules are by making a few phone calls to reporters who cover your organization. Just ask.

On the other hand, there are exceptions or gray areas, I suppose, in a journalist accepting gifts during the course of doing a story. The story about Mike Wallace of the CBS "60 Minutes" news program and Washington, D.C., philanthropist Catherine Reynolds is an example that jumps out.

"60 Minutes" decided to do a story about Reynolds, who had been the target of numerous local newspaper stories about her fight with the Smithsonian Institution. She admits she had "caused some controversy in the musty, stodgy gentlemen's club of philanthropy."

Reynolds created a fortune by turning around a failing student loan company. Then, as the head of the philanthropic Catherine B. Reynolds Foundation, she gave away millions of dollars to charities and the arts. A few years ago, Reynolds offered $38 million to the Smithsonian Institution, but when she and the Smithsonian couldn't agree on how the money would be spent, she withdrew the gift and turned her generosity toward the Kennedy Center in Washington.

So Mike Wallace and a "60 Minutes" camera crew decided to follow Ms. Reynolds around for a few days and find out something about this new benefactor on the Washington scene and what she was up to. Following her around included accompanying her on a trip to Europe aboard a luxury corporate jet she had hired.

There are still some unanswered questions about whether she and her husband would have flown in such lavish style had Wallace and his crew not been along. I am convinced it was an intelligently planned set-up to manipulate Wallace, you can only draw our own conclusions. But everyone flew to London aboard a Gulfstream IV business jet and it was first-class treatment from Reynolds and her husband all the way for Wallace, his producer, his camera crew, and a couple of public relations consultants.

And just to make sure everyone had a good time, the CBS News folks were presented with digital cameras among the gifts from Ms. Reynolds and her husband.

At this point you might be wondering what kind of story the occasionally sharp-elbowed Wallace, famous for his "ambush" style of TV news, did on Reynolds. Well, it was an extremely favorable feature and nothing like all the other stories written about her. In fact, the two of them got along "fabulously," as someone close to the story shared with me, and it showed on the air.

Prior to agreeing to do the story with "60 Minutes," Reynolds had hired a major public relations agency to frame just the right story angle, feeling, and environment to win over and control "60 Minutes" coverage, and it worked.

Let me point out that the hard-hitting days of "ambush" investigative journalism at "60 Minutes" ended well over a decade ago. The attack-dog style tended to make viewers uncomfortable and advertisers squeamish. Mike Wallace and his pals on "60 Minutes" are more feature-oriented today, less controversial by design.

Knowing Wallace's once-edgy type of reporting had softened in his senior years, the public relations experts did their homework. They skillfully crafted an approach that would play to his interest in helping the underdog.

Coached and briefed, Reynolds appeared to Wallace as a successful businesswoman—which she was—who had been unfairly harassed by old guard society when she was just a generous philanthropist who only wanted to help improve some of America's most respected cultural institutions. It was that story that appeared on "60 Minutes;" the string of negative stories in the local media ended after such powerful national exposure.

Riding on the Gulfstream and receiving the cameras didn't hurt the news crew's opinion of Reynolds. After all, CBS could have said no to the gifts and royal treatment, in keeping with long-standing CBS corporate policy. A former CBS News correspondent in Washington told me they should have responded, "Hell, no!" to the gifts.

On the other hand, the luxury is OK with their bosses if a news crew can make a ride on a private jet part of the story. For example, shooting a little snippet of video of Reynolds while in the air en route to London makes everything just fine, I suppose.

Wallace's warm and fuzzy defending of Ms. Reynolds subsequently earned him invitations to become a permanent fixture in Washington society events sponsored by the clever philanthropist. The intelligent PR people she hired effectively proved how easy it is to control the media, even a major story on CBS "60 Minutes."

Flying the media to Europe aboard private jets and digital

cameras as gifts aside, more appropriate, affordable, and realistic gifts to the media may present a challenge that can rival the creative thought you invest in developing an imaginative story pitch and supporting background materials in the first place. I have seen some public relations agencies actually spend more time trying to figure out what gifts to give the media than on the messages and image they hope to see in print.

PR stunts are also fraught with hazard. There was an infamous incident in the 1990s when cardboard boxes with air holes in them started turning up at newspaper offices all over London. The journalists to whom they were addressed opened them to find live pigeons inside—a PR stunt designed to draw attention to a new investment product. The parcel came with instructions to release the pigeons outside.

The stunt backfired spectacularly—the animal-rights lobbyists went on the warpath—and the PR agency that cooked up the stunt lost the account.

The technology industry has been among the most ineffective in handling media relations, largely because of the limited scope of experience and creativity among the young people doing PR in that business. Despite all the useful new ideas in technology, the industry as a whole does a pretty unimaginative job when it comes to promoting itself, most often copying some old idea or something a competitor is trying.

Not only is the tech industry T-shirt crazy, but if I've seen one "stress ball" or coffee mug imprinted with the name of a tech outfit, I've seen a hundred of them.

Once a technology high-flyer known for giving out stress balls and coffee mugs to reporters, tried a slightly different approach and handed out samples of their information technology product on a compact disc for journalists. When inserted into a computer, however, the CD caused the computer to crash and resulted in corrupted files and damage that required hours to correct. Imagine the aggravation to a reporter who relied on the computer to finish a story. A marketing person apologetically said that there had been a "glitch" in the software for the media. No kidding.

There are people, however, whom I would consider masters of the universe when it comes to stunts that capture valuable and influential media attention and drive home a message. Sir Richard Branson of Virgin Group is at the top of my list and earns my respect and admiration for his consistent integrity, jet-set hipness, courage, and sheer guts.

Branson does not fly hot-air balloons around the world solely because he necessarily likes to fly balloons. He does it because daredevil stunts like that are the best free advertising for his brand in the world. He knows how to break out of competitive clutter, using the media.

He is a one-man publicity machine—recognized as an authentic, self-made international mogul and bon vivant—and his corporate empire has thrived, for the most part, because of his brilliant leadership. He is a master at manipulating the press to get sensational coverage but no one seems to care. Branson is so darn considerate and likeable. Even some of his business failures have become legend among journalists.

Reporters in New York still remember Sir Richard arriving in Times Square atop an Army tank to promote his new Virgin Cola—an event that happened years ago and is better remembered than his cola, which flopped! The tank signified challenging the competition and moving into new territory, similar to the approach Branson took when his Virgin Atlantic challenged British Airways and American Airlines on trans-Atlantic routes. Guess where the photo event took place? Right in front of Branson's Virgin Record store in Manhattan. Talk about brilliant cross-promoting of a brand!

It all worked together. Everything Branson and his Virgin Group used to promote the event was relevant to the occasion, as is always the case. Everything was first-class. The event was bold almost to the point of being outrageous but of course, it was in New York, right?

Branson is master over 350 Virgin-branded companies, and it is his individual image and voice that brings each of them to life to capture terrific media coverage with the magnificent grace and timing of a symphony conductor.

Branson's hype to launch Virgin America in 2007—his skillful entry into the hotly competitive and political U.S. air carrier territory—included personally bringing TV comic and Comedy Central faux news commentator Stephen Colbert along on the New York to San Francisco inaugural flight, thus generating great photo opportunities.

When I was head of global corporate communications at Gulfstream Aerospace, I always questioned the relevance and purpose of promotional materials that we gave to the news media. I never wanted to distract from a pitch by sending anything other than background material that was focused on getting the story—no extraneous gifts or trinkets that might possibly derail our goal of getting a story.

I had the ultimate promotional tool at my disposal that no one else on earth had—not even Sir Richard Branson. I had an ultra long-range Gulfstream V business jet, an aircraft that could fly higher—50,000 feet—and farther—6,500 nautical miles—than most other aircraft in service. It is the most elegant and certainly the sexiest business jet in the sky, a symbol of achievement and success. My responsibility was to introduce the Gulfstream V to the world and build prominent visibility to attract customers.

Gulfstream, like other business aircraft manufacturers, had previously promoted its planes in the aviation trade publications and had, as a result, gotten lost in all the competitive clutter. They had for years sent out news releases and press kits to the trades, just as everyone else was doing, and it had not moved the needle toward generating widespread media coverage. Gulfstream had never considered that the mainstream media might consider their story to be appealing, and so they had not tried.

I took a completely different approach and did something unheard of in the aircraft business. Corporate CEOs and wealthy individuals, the people who can afford to buy a $40 million Gulfstream V, don't read aviation trades. They read the mainstream media. I took the Gulfstream V mainstream, to where the customers are, and it worked like a charm.

Snagging front-page coverage in papers from Los Angeles to Brussels to Beijing to Johannesburg required a lot of free rides for a lot of reporters. And what a perk it was! When I took the first Gulfstream V aircraft on world demo tours, I would contact feature and business reporters in advance for major stories to alert them that the Gulfstream V was coming to their town. At first, their reaction was, "So what?"

Then, I would offer a brief flight that would take them up to an altitude of 50,000 feet, up above all other aircraft traffic, where the sky is nearly cobalt blue, and you can clearly see the curvature of the earth. No one declined. Then I would say that the only catch was that I hoped they would write at least part of their story while at 50,000 feet. Everyone agreed.

To contrast the exclusivity of riding aboard a Gulfstream V, I kept it simple by giving each reporter who flew with us up to 50,000 feet a top-quality blue ball cap—the same kind as worn by Gulfstream's test pilots—embroidered "Gulfstream V—World Tour." Was the ball cap an imaginative idea as a gift? Well, I've seen better. Was it relative to the event? You bet! Only those people who flew on the aircraft got a cap. I know of some journalists who, years later, still covet those hats, because they can still boast of flying in a GV to an altitude of 50,000, nearly the edge of space. It was simple and classy and relevant, and it worked.

When I pitched a *Business Week* correspondent on doing a cover story about Theodore Forstmann, the investor who owned Gulfstream at the time, the part of the deal that clinched the story was a commitment to shuttle the reporter around on a Gulfstream as he gathered background for his story. The reporter actually asked for the rides to … sort of, kind of … get a feel for traveling in the lap of luxury. Forget the flight cap—the rides worked and a favorable cover story was in the bag, guaranteed.

There is a similarity between the countless media rides that I staged aboard a new Gulfstream V with how CBS "60 Minutes" was given a first-class flight to London with Catherine B. Reynolds. I used the tactic to build much greater global awareness in order to differentiate an expensive and special business aircraft from competitors, and to generate mainstream media coverage that was unprecedented in the business aviation industry. The goal was to sell airplanes. Ms. Reynolds used the exclusive environment within a trans-Atlantic Gulfstream flight to establish a bond of friendship with Mike Wallace that clearly influenced his story on "60 Minutes."

By promoting the Gulfstream V prominently with clever stories in the mainstream news media while all other business aircraft companies focused entirely on the narrow reach of the aerospace industry trade publications, we were able to reposition the brand of a Gulfstream jet as the hallmark of business aviation.

It happened through a strategy of shifting corporate focus outward to emphasize the merits of Gulfstream as a corporate tool for business success; the tactic used the mainstream news media to carry the message directly to corporate executives, wealthy individuals, and important decision-makers around the world. Gulfstream has become, as a result, the most coveted ride in the sky.

The results were dramatic—orders for the Gulfstream V jumped, sales increased by more than 400 percent, and the company went public through a highly successful over-subscribed initial public offering (IPO).

The rules and boundaries for a journalist accepting a gift are ever-shifting and defined and self-imposed by each news organization. It's not determined by government regulations or mandated by industry rules. Most professional news organizations have established clear policies for their employees that set limits on what constitutes a token gift and what is bribery or payola —and therefore forbidden. The rules vary from one news organization to another. So if you have a question about gift giving, don't assume. It's always best to ask first and avoid a possible awkward situation with a journalist.

There's nothing wrong with using *trash and trinkets*—within ethical limits—to drive home a promotional message as long as the campaign is imaginative, savvy and, most of all, relevant to the story. Sometimes, you might get lucky and offer a special perk or exclusive benefit that can be experienced by the media in the course of covering your story. You will be surprised by how that most often results in favorable media coverage. Just ask Mike Wallace.

CHAPTER THIRTY-FIVE

SAVVY MEDIA COVERAGE IS NOT ROCKET SCIENCE

Let us delve a little deeper into what is involved in making great media coverage happen. Chief executives who consistently stand in the media's spotlight to talk about their organizations and themselves recognize they have more clout and authority than their PR people, and they use it. Media savvy CEOs who have invested the time in building meaningful media contacts can always get the right journalist on the telephone or reply promptly to an e-mail. These leaders always control a media situation more effectively; they do not rely on PR people who may or may not have the right contacts and access.

People in the media want direct access to newsmakers, not necessarily intermediaries. Most journalists are sophisticated enough to know how to treat, respect, and keep high-level news sources by not burning bridges.

Forget all the talk about whether to have a CEO blog or podcast, the largest media list in the galaxy, or the fattest media kit. Those things are trivial and actually create barriers to an executive effectively leading an organization's brand and vision. The return-on-investment is questionable in a world that's built on relationships.

"Nothing counts for more than relationship and knowledge," John Pletz of the Texas-based *Austin American-Statesman* told me. "The best pitches I get are from people who know our publication, what we cover, who we cover, and how we like to cover it. Don't over think it. It's not rocket science.

"I like to talk about the way technology changes people's lives, that I'm interested in the personalities of people who create great and groundbreaking stuff (and how they did it, and how it works), and that when I write about companies I'm into the narrative of their struggles."

Michael Rosenbaum, a producer at CBS "60 Minutes," suggested that if you call him about story, provide an anecdote or two that might illuminate the issue. It's one thing to suggest a story, it's quite another to find a way to bring it to life, supported by appealing visuals.

Newsweek's technology reporter Steven Levy readily shared his game book on how to pitch him with a good story that might make it into the weekly magazine.

"It's not so much about some original pitch," he said. "Do your homework and know the publication and the reporter you are pitching, making damn sure that what you are representing is something that would logically be written by that reporter for that publication.

"For our newsroom, short e-mails work best," said Lisa Mullins, anchor and senior producer of BBC's "The World."

"Right now, there's a stack of pitches that have come over our fax machine in the last few days. About five percent will get looked at. Maybe faxes work well in some newsrooms. Not in ours. So it's best to find out the preferred, most efficient method of making your pitch.

"I don't expect people to know precisely how a journalist works, but the more they know, the better," Mullins counseled.

Timing can be everything in landing good media coverage of your story. Broadcast producer and journalist Pat Piper said, "Anticipate. Know when a congressional committee is going to schedule a hearing, and get out there ahead of it. Know when an anniversary of some sort is coming, and get out in front of it."

Most of all, practice openness and transparency in what you say. Journalists know which organizations have reputations for communicating accurately with the media, and which do not.

Richard Serrano of the *Los Angeles Times* says the best organizations "are those who are honest and forthright with information, willing to steer you to the right aspect of a story without compromising their side. The worst are those who refuse to comment or cooperate and end up actually hurting their client or organization."

Effective strategic communications today is built on a foundation of respect, trust, and a working relationship with reporters who have an interest in your organization and your story. It requires staying disciplined, a learning of what the media needs for a news story, keeping up to date on what specific reporters are writing, and adding a healthy dose of good timing.

By being attuned to today's style of storytelling to generate media coverage and how the news business works from a journalist's perspective— whether mainstream journalism or New Media—an organization can enjoy accurate news coverage that is credible and influential toward achieving whatever goals you establish or can imagine.

CHAPTER THIRTY-SIX

FACING THE WOLF PACK

Much of this book has focused on communications techniques from a journalist's perspective that will show a media savvy leader and executive how to better communicate their visions and messages through the powerful conduit of the media. I have written a good deal on understanding how journalists approach their jobs and what elements need to come together to create legitimate news.

If you want to achieve outstanding coverage by the media—whether a daily newspaper, cable news, or an online news site—it only makes sense to speak their language. This understanding of the news media will give you a competitive edge and prepare you to speak with the media.

An interview with the news media can occur any time and any place. An interview can be planned or occur spontaneously, without warning. An interview may result because you have called a contact at the local newspaper with a good, timely story about your organization—or because the telephone rings and a reporter at the other end of the line is asking for just a few minutes of your time to answer some questions.

Either way, the primary objective of effective strategic communications is to communicate the story you want to tell as clearly and accurately as possible in a controlled way that helps ensure good publicity for you or your organization.

The job of a reporter is to ferret out a story that will be of interest to readers, listeners, or viewers.

An interview is not a conversation. It is a ritual in which the reporter seeks a news story, sometimes based on a preconceived notion, and you deliver focused messages that credibly tell your story. You want good coverage; the reporter wants news. Remember, it's not a conversation.

One of the most important rules is to avoid being interviewed when you are tired or angry. During Hurricane Katrina in 2005, we saw an exhausted and often angry Mayor C. Ray Nagin saying to reporters that 10,000 people had died in New Orleans. He didn't know how many people had died, and we all knew he was guessing. And, he was guessing wrong.

Sure, he had every right to be angry at the incompetence and lack of timely responsive by the federal government, and many of us sympathized, but it didn't help Nagin's credibility when he vented his fury, using profanity, on radio rather than in phone calls to Washington. As mayor of a major city who had been thrust into the world media spotlight, he had the responsibility to communicate accurate news, not guesses or anger, and he fumbled.

Never guess when you don't know.

It's also important to know when to stop talking, especially about issues outside of your area of expertise. It's important to know when to shut up.

Cindy Sheehan, the brokenhearted mother who had lost her son Casey to the Iraq war in 2004, had the world on her side when she camped outside President George W. Bush's ranch in Texas, seeking to meet with the president. The more Bush ignored her, the more sympathetic media coverage she got, until she started answering questions about Israel and Palestine, a completely different and complex subject about which she knew nothing.

The lesson is to limit your area of expertise and remember a quote often attributed to Grover Cleveland, the former President of the United States, who said, "I never got in trouble with things I didn't say." Incidentally, it is nearly impossible to confirm whether Cleveland actually said that or whether it is myth. Regardless, it is a good adage to remember.

When Sheehan stepped outside her circle of knowledge, conservative bloggers—many of the same people who attacked presidential hopeful John Kerry in 2004—quickly went on the attack against her with a deluge of harsh quotable quotes for the media and a smear campaign, including a claim that she was disgracing her dead son's legacy "by serving as a pawn for well-organized, anti-American activist groups." Bloggers said Sheehan "is a willing poster child for radical left-wing America haters … is using her son's death … is cruelly robbing our fallen soldiers of the high honor that they deserve …."

If you are not convinced yet of the power of blogs to influence the media, all you need to do is Google what happened to Kerry and Sheehan as a result of these vicious attacks by mostly invisible bloggers who got the media's attention, primarily because someone knew how to craft a quotable quote—the sort of clever, short phrase that reporters love for their stories.

Blogs, interactive content management platforms, dynamic RSS, newsreaders, and other emerging technology are being used as positive and constructive tools of strategic communications, as I have discussed earlier in this book.

Here's a list of interview dos and don'ts that I have observed from many years as a network news correspondent and then as a strategic communications agency executive.

First, the things you can do in an interview:

- *Always remember: It's your agenda.* You do an interview not to help out a reporter but to communicate a positive message or image about your organization. Set your own boundaries. If a reporter calls out of the blue for an interview, you are under no obligation to drop everything and give an interview at that moment. Explain that you are finishing up something and will call the reporter back in 30 minutes. Ask about the subject he or she wants to discuss. Never ask for a list of specific questions, because this compromises the working ethics of journalism. Thus, starting off on the wrong foot. Then take 30 minutes or so to focus on what you want to say and communicate in the interview. This time will also help settle nerves that many people experience when contacted by the news media.

- *Always think three.* Think of three messages you want to communicate in the interview. Think of how to deliver each message in an interesting and concise way. This is the core of what you want to communicate in the interview so be prepared to stick with these messages. Memorize them.

By having three messages, you can enhance control of an interview by providing depth and perspective. One message is emotional in nature, such as a shared human experience. One message is logical; "it only makes sense." And one message is analytical, backing up your other messages with facts and data. These three messages—emotional, logical, and analytical—work together to present your side in the most compelling and controllable manner possible. This tactic boosts your chances of controlling the interview and landing a good story.

- *Always seek opportunities to bridge to your three points.* A *bridge* is an interview tactic to control and redirect an interview back to the subject that you want to talk about. If the reporter asks a question, for example, that is far afield from what you want to talk about, no problem. Acknowledge the reporter by answering the question briefly and then bridge back to your messages. A bridge can be just a few words, such as, "I believe one of the most important things to remember is ..." or, "We need to keep in mind that ..." And then get back on track with your messages. Remember, it's your interview so make the most of it.

- *Always anticipate all questions.* When you know in advance that a reporter is doing an interview, you can do a little online research on other stories the reporter has written and can get a good feel for what questions will be asked. Never go into an interview without first making a list of questions, even tough questions, you believe a reporter might ask. Ask colleagues to join in this exercise. It's a good way to quickly rehearse what you might say in an interview. If you wing it, you are headed for trouble and may lose any chance for control of the interview and the outcome you desire.

- *Always know when to stop.* The best answer to a reporter's question is a concise answer. The shorter the answer, the better. I cannot tell you the hundreds of times I have heard a reporter ask a question that deserves just a 30-second response but receives a five-minute answer that makes the reporter's eyes glaze over. It's like asking someone what time it is and then they build you a clock. As a general rule, keep answers to 30 seconds or less during a broadcast interview and to a minute or less in an interview with the print media. If a reporter thinks a certain answer is too short, he or she can always ask a follow-up question.

- *Always answer the question you were asked.* Listen to each question. Answer that question. Interviews are stressful enough without attempting to interpret or analyze what you think the reporter's motives might be. If you don't like the direction of a question, answer it briefly and bridge back to your own talking points.

- *Always try to use quotable quotes.* Use colloquialisms, quote someone famous, or use a memorable play on words, if appropriate, to make your point. Reporters love quotable quotes. Such quotes can make you look good in an interview and control the direction of the story.

- *Always back up message points with statistics and facts.* When you use credible data to make your point in an interview, you earn respect and credibility.

- *Always remember that how you say it is as important as what you say.* In an interview, be genuine and sincere. Take some time before an interview to—as they say—get yourself in a good place. Go into an interview with a positive frame of mind. Don't be afraid to smile. Use your voice, eyes, and expressions to show passion in your words.

- *Always maintain eye contact.* Whether in a newspaper or television interview, look at the reporter, and never allow your eyes to stray. Don't sneak a glance at the camera lens or someone standing nearby. Eye contact tells a reporter that this interview is the most important thing you are doing right now. If your eyes wander during a television interview, the perception may be that you are nervous.

- *Always remember that a microphone is always on.* Never say anything silly or inappropriate assuming a microphone has been switched off. It can happen to anyone. Back in the 1980s, then-president Ronald Reagan, an old pro with the media who should have known better, jokingly said, "We start bombing Russia in five minutes." A microphone was on and Reagan's playful remark made embarrassing headlines around the world.

- *Always briefly summarize your key points at the end of the interview.* You have the forum—the spotlight—so make the most of it. A summary provides you with a final opportunity to deliver your three messages, again.

Now, for a short list of things to avoid doing in an interview:

- *Never talk off the record.* It kills your credibility with the news media.

- *Never say anything you don't want to see in print or on the air.* If you are angry with someone or a situation, don't use the interview as a forum to say something casually on the side that you don't think a reporter will hear or use. An interview is not a time to kid around.

- *Never take it personally or get defensive.* Reporters, in most cases, are just out doing their job of finding news stories. Work with them and everyone wins. The days of ambush journalism ended years ago.

- *Never assume an interview is a conversation.* There is nothing casual or chatty about an interview, no matter how informal a particular reporter's style might be. A reporter is always working to find a good story.

- *Never make up answers.* If you don't know, say so and promise to get the information and respond promptly.

So often when someone claims he or she has been misquoted in an interview, it's because of something the interviewee said. An apparent misquote usually happens because the person being interviewed has said something contradictory or ambiguous, even though the journalist usually and wrongfully gets the blame. It happens often because the interviewee simply talked too much.

The same guidelines apply for doing television or radio interviews except there are the added distractions of microphones, lights, and cameras. No problem. Here is a simple crib sheet I've used for years with clients to help them control broadcast interviews and communicate clear and persuasive messages:

- Be accessible to reporters.

- Tell the truth.

- For TV and radio interviews, modulate your voice to avoid sounding monotone and possibly dull.

- Be prepared. If you don't know the issue inside and out, find a colleague who does and have them do the interview. If they turn out to be terrified of the microphone, have them thoroughly brief you, giving you more information than you need to get the organization's story and position across.

- When asked a question, get to the point quickly. This is perhaps the most important tip when doing a broadcast interview—*get to the point quickly.*

- Never use 27 words when four will do.

- If you are doing a television interview with other people, act as if the camera is always focused on you, whether or not you are speaking or being spoken to.

- In a studio setting with an interviewer or even several people, look at the person who is asking you questions—not at the camera. Don't stare off into space.

- If you're on a panel, really listen to what the other people are saying and look interested while they are talking … because the camera might be on you.

The latest technology has created opportunities for doing live TV interviews from remote locations, including from your own office.

For corporate, non-profit and academic organizations that do frequent live TV appearances, it is no longer necessary for an expert spokesperson to take valuable time to travel to TV studios. VideoLink (VideoLink.tv) is a Boston-based company that connects a growing list of clients with the TV news media by providing remotely controlled broadcast-quality cameras and all the support necessary for an organization to increase its television exposure.

One VideoLink client is the Capital Markets Group of Stifel Nicolaus, a financial services company, in Baltimore, Maryland. When a TV business news program calls for a live interview with a Stifel Nicolaus analyst—whose time means money—the financial expert simply walks a few steps to the in-house VideoLink camera for the interview. VideoLink coordinates camera operation and handles the technical details with the TV news program.

It's a popular trend particularly among cable television news program where producers, under tight budgets, now have a way to get timely and relevant interviews with experts at little or no cost, and with little advance notice. Companies, like Stifel Nicolaus, can showcase expertise and receive national brand exposure.

As you might expect, how you look on television—your style of clothing, posture, expressions, and hand gestures—is nearly as important as what you have to say. Your appearance helps to build credibility.

- Wear clothes that will not distract people from what you are saying; fairly conservative business attire in mostly solid colors are often most appropriate. Incidentally, men no longer need to wear blue shirts for TV interviews because of today's high-quality cameras. Yet the color of what you wear can work to send subtle and influential signals to an audience. For example, when Vice President Dick Cheney gave his first television interview about the hunting accident in which he blasted Texas attorney Harry Whittington with birdshot from his shotgun, Cheney was dressed in a dark suit and pink tie. A red tie is part of Cheney's signature business attire, but in the environment of accepting responsibility for shooting someone, red would make too bold and authoritative a statement. Pink, on the other hand, is the color of innocence and warmth. Clearly the vice president's pink tie worked to his favor.

- If being interviewed while standing, stand up straight. Slouching can send a message of being bored or having a negative attitude.

- If giving at interview while seated, sit up straight. If at a table, lean in slightly to show that you are engaged in providing honest answers. People who slouch back in their chairs during interviews can send a signal, right or wrong, of arrogance.

- It's helpful to learn something about TV makeup in case the guys interviewing you don't have someone there to powder your nose or forehead.

- Avoid waving your hands around during a television interview. It's distracting and might make you appear like someone in a used-car commercial or one of today's crop of overly dramatic TV reporters. If you want to make a point with a hand gesture, do so with one hand and in meaningful movements.

- If doing a TV interview from a remote location, where you are talking only to a camera, such as the VideoLink example, look right at the camera lens at all times. Remember that the audience is viewing you through that camera so focus on talking to the lens.

- Look natural and friendly, but don't smile at the interviewer while you're talking about something serious.

Newsmakers I have coached have been guided by these simple rules when facing cameras and microphones, often during impromptu and high-pressure situations. The ability to master the protocol of broadcast interviews has allowed them to focus on their words and messages they want to deliver. As a result, that credibility has helped build many enduring relationships with journalists.

Lastly, if you are ambushed by a surprise question, heed the advice of former Secretary of Defense Robert S. McNamara: Just answer the question you *wish* had been asked.

People who have mastered the discipline of being interviewed and talking with journalists on a high level of mutual respect and trust, know the effectiveness of using the news media as an enormously powerful and influential communication tool to reach vast and important audiences. Those people are today's leaders.

Chapter Thirty-Seven heading

CHAPTER THIRTY-SEVEN

THE BEST MARKETING WEAPON

Our world is dominated by the media—newspapers, blogs, online news and information, television, cable TV channels, radio, satellite, wireless ... the list seemingly expands every week. The media's power to influence opinions and perceptions is staggering. We are bombarded each day by information as never before.

The challenge of today's authentic leader is to know how to cut through all of the competitive message clutter to attract the spotlight of media attention, and then, know how to frame vision, ideas, and words into appealing messages. Those few individuals who invest the time to polish the skills are instantly heard and recognized.

It is all about communicating effectively through the news media, using contemporary techniques that will help your organization's news and messages prominently reach the right audiences at the right time while making the right impression.

An organization cannot build such credibility by purchasing a display advertisement on the front page of a major daily newspaper in America. That newspaper real estate isn't for sale. Yet it is possible for that organization to achieve outstanding coverage, not only on the front page but also on today's equally influential online news sites. Effective strategic communications is the most powerful weapon in an organization's marketing arsenal.

Over the years, I have witnessed political greatness defined, such as the image of Ronald Reagan, through strategic communications, guided by people of intellect, integrity, and media smarts, like my former colleague and friend, the late Michael Deaver.

Deaver was vice chairman of Edelman Worldwide in Washington, D.C. In one of many communications initiatives, he guided a media blitz that sent the report by the National Commission on Terrorist Attacks Upon the United States by the September 11 Commission skyrocketing to the top of national bestseller lists, resulting in a nomination for a National Book Award. The media campaign influenced Congress, the administration, and key liberal and conservative influencers to embrace the commission's findings upon release.

The blanket of media coverage that was generated reached across the country and around the world. As a result of the coverage, the commission's Web site received more than 50 million hits in the first 24 hours. Throughout the coverage, the message the Commission wanted to deliver to America was clear and used plain language.

You see, more often than not, such high levels of media coverage doesn't just happen by accident; *it is made to happen* by skilled communications leaders and pros with extensive contacts among journalists.

My own work in media relations has centered on enhancing the competitive positioning, brand image, and reputations of corporations. Many times I have worked with clients to devise persuasive messages and to sell products through the powerful clout in the news media.

One of my most memorable experiences happened when London Records asked me to find a way to propel sales of compact discs for the first Three Tenors Concert, which was about to happen in July of that year. London Records saw it as another opera recording, and that was a real challenge—opera recordings are not hot-selling items in America.

The company's top executives had set a seemingly unattainable sales goal of 200,000 CDs during the first two months of the recording's release. It appeared to be an impossible task since the previously biggest selling opera recording in America had sold just 50,000 CDs over three years.

So off I flew to Rome to attend the concert and look for a story angle to pitch to the news media that would make news and publicize the recording in order to stimulate sales.

As I sat in the audience beside legendary coloratura soprano

Beverly Sills, watching Luciano Pavarotti, José Carreras, and Plácido Domingo's amazing performance on a stage in the ancient Baths of Caracalla along the Appian Way in Rome, an idea struck me. This was not an opera performance as much as it was a *historic event*, a never before happening. And that made all the difference in the world in successfully positioning it before the news media.

The royalty, celebrities, and social elite of Europe had come together not for an opera concert, but because they recognized history in the making. Pavarotti, Carreras, and Domingo, all revered stars, had never before performed together on the same stage and it was making headlines around the world, except in the United States.

Once back home, I made quiet soundings among friends and contacts in the national news media to find someone who might be interested in the story. The initial reaction was as if *opera* were a five-letter dirty word. No one had heard of the concert and no one really cared—no one except Cindy Carpien, the much-adored producer of National Public Radio's "Weekend Edition" with Scott Simon on Saturdays.

Cindy was intrigued by the fact that she hadn't heard of such a big event. There had not been one mention of it in the U.S. news media. Over a period of about a week, we talked several times to figure out how the story could be told on radio. It didn't seem feasible to interview only one of the tenors without the others, but to get all three together for such an interview would be impossible. So I proposed an interview with someone who had worked individually with each of the three tenors for 20 years and finally had the chance to work with all three together—the English recording engineer, James Locke. Cindy agreed.

Locke was a colorful interviewee. As excerpts from the first Three Tenors recording were played on NPR, he described the "magic" that filled the air that evening in Rome.

He painted a verbal picture for the radio audience that allowed listeners to experience what that evening of music was like amid the setting at the 3rd century Baths of Caracalla and the historic pines of Rome. His vivid descriptions took listeners there and provided a behind-the-scenes glimpse of the event and who attended. Not once did he mention the word *opera*, but instead he described why the *historic event* had brought thousands of people together in Rome.

The piece ran 12 minutes on a Saturday morning and was heard on nearly 400 NPR stations by an audience in the millions, primarily baby boomers—a generation that enjoys an appealing new trend.

Within a week, all 200,000 CDs of the first Three Tenors Concert recording were sold. It was the power of one cleverly developed story angle on a radio news program that was heard by the right audience. The recording went on to be the biggest-selling classical CD in history.

I wrote no news releases, no fact sheets, no media kits. The story happened by making phone calls to established contacts in the news media and working with them to develop an angle and provide someone to interview. As we've said elsewhere in this book, it's all about relationships and understanding how the media works.

Balanced and accurate news media coverage of a business or organization creates lasting goodwill, boosts an image, sells products, and enhances credible influence more effectively than any other kind of mass communication. It will help to build a brand with enduring credibility.

Good communications helps an organization break out of competitive clutter. It really doesn't matter whether you are the largest or number one. If the media likes you and is captivated by what you say, then you are perceived as a leader.

News in today's world is reported literally every minute, 'round the clock, via the traditional channels of newspapers, wire services, magazines, television, and radio—but also through Web sites, social networking sites online, blogs, and an ever-increasing variety of online sources that are evolving in today's digital revolution.

But despite the diversity of today's types of media, the most effective communications comes down to getting to know the right journalists and what they need to do their jobs, understanding what is news and what isn't, and working together with reporters on a professional and trusted level to provide the background information, facts, and interviews they need to make a story happen.

And all along the way, those executives and corporate leaders who communicate the unique vision of their organizations must be able to express enthusiasm without sounding like publicists. Clear and credible messages in everyday plain language must be crafted and neatly tucked inside the context of legitimate news. Clever and contemporary communications techniques, consistently and professionally managed, will deliver impressive results and make news. The competitive leadership and enhanced corporate or organizational value and influence that results from great news media coverage can be the stuff of legends.

Praise for *The Media Savvy Leader* and David Henderson

In the Internet age, executives have to learn how to shape information about themselves and their companies, or the Internet will do it for them, and it won't be pretty. **— Mark Cuban**
Billionaire Entrepreneur, Chairman of HDNet Television,
and Owner of the Dallas Mavericks

Among the attributes of leadership, the ability to communicate clearly has never been more important that it is today. If you want to become a more effective communicator, David Henderson has the experience and the skills to help.
— Dan Rather
Television News Anchor and Journalist

David Henderson knows what we journalists know: the more that news and information saturate our society, the more savvy and discriminating the media and their audiences become. An executive wanting to communicate effectively must be honest and real. David's got the skill, the experience, and the instincts to help you find your authentic voice. **— Lisa Mullins**
Anchor, Public Radio International/BBC's *The World*

To be an effective leader today, you must reach the hearts and minds and keyboards and eyeballs of your consumers and employees in a way that is true, authentic, and meaningful. This book details—in an easy-to-digest manner—how to do so, and to thine own self be true. **— Ted Leonsis**
Vice Chairman Emeritus of AOL and Owner of Washington Capitals

Great advice and a much-needed reality check for anyone who works with the media. Follow David's guidelines and save yourself a lot of time and energy.
— Jean Cochran
Morning Edition, National Public Radio

David Henderson shares insight and real-life examples to help executives get media attention and communicate the vision of their organizations. Most PR 'experts' do it one way. David's techniques are different and get results. **— Gary Shapiro**
CEO of Consumer Electronics Association